D0572698

Just Three Things

Just Three Things

Bite-Size Ways to Transform Your Life

Linda Bonnar

This edition was published by The Dreamwork Collective
The Dreamwork Collective LLC, Dubai, United Arab Emirates
thedreamworkcollective.com

Printed and bound in the United Arab Emirates
Cover and design: Dania Zafar

Text © Linda Bonnar, 2021

ISBN 978-9948-8719-6-5

Approved by National Media Council Dubai, United Arab Emirates
MC-02-01-4358097

All rights reserved. No part of this publication may be reproduced, stored, or transmitted in any form or by any means, electronic, mechanical, photo-copying, recording, or otherwise, without prior permission of the publishers. The right of Linda Bonnar to be identified as the author of this work has been asserted and protected under the UAE Copyright and Authorship Protection Law No. 7.

Contents

Introduction

'This seems like a lot, Linda,' my client said as he looked at the list of five things he had come up with to work on before our next session. 'Not sure if five things is realistic to get done before next week, to be honest.'

'Okay, tell me what does seem realistic?' I asked.

'I can do... those three... Yup, three is good. Anyone can do three, right?' He laughed. 'But five? Five is pushing it.'

And he was right. Anyone can do three things, right? After all, it's *just* three things. Three sounds doable; it sounds manageable, simple, and effective.

I had my book.

Welcome to *Just Three Things*.

Whether you're seeking to create change in your personal life or you're looking to develop professionally, this book is for you. From developing more self-confidence and managing stress, to letting go of your past and dealing with overwhelm, *Just Three Things* equips you with a variety of tips, tools, and techniques to help you overcome challenges to get the results you want. We'll explore ways of developing better habits, managing your thoughts, and navigating change to bring about positive transformation in your life with bite-size actions.

I wrote this book because I know what it's like to want to make changes—big changes. I know what it's like to feel stuck, to feel frustrated with the way things are and completely lost as to how to turn them around. I know how scary change can be (*What if I fail?*) and how overwhelming it can be too (*I don't even know where to start!*). It's no wonder we don't welcome change with open arms.

But I also know how incredible change can be. Despite the fear, the pain, and all the other discomfort change can bring, what an absolutely amazing feeling it is to look back and see how far you've come.

This book is designed to make the process of change more manageable for you. Inside, you'll find a whole range of coaching tips, techniques, and strategies to help you successfully overcome the challenges you're facing and move forward confidently with your life.

When it comes to creating change in our lives, we literally need just three things to begin.

1. We have to want to create the change.
2. We need to know what we want instead.
3. We need to know how to bring about that change—even if it's just the first step.

As long as you want to see change, you're ready to begin.

Welcome to *Just Three Things*. I'm delighted you're here.

How to use this book

Unlike many of the books that grace our bookshelves or coffee tables (or even hold our coffee tables up!) and never get a second glance after they've been read once, *Just Three Things* is different. It doesn't want to be read cover to cover and then used as a coaster or table leg; it wants to be like your favourite Netflix series or your go-to feel-good movie—it wants to be revisited over and over again! It wants to be underlined and highlighted, covered in sticky notes and Post-its that draw your attention back to those important mental reminders when you need them the most. Use this book to learn something new about yourself and about others. Use this book to help you understand how to apply that new learning. Use this book to build better relationships, better habits, and better behaviours.

Just Three Things has been designed to equip you with the skills you need to successfully overcome the challenges you're facing today and those that might show up tomorrow. Each chapter focuses on one particular topic, for example how to navigate change or how to deal with impostor syndrome. Each chapter is then divided into three sections: three different ways of approaching this one problem, three simple and manageable ways you can deal with the challenge you're facing.

At the end of each section, you'll find both an Action Step and a Further Thoughts section. The Action Step is the quick win you can take away with you and do now, with this book still in hand! It's that first step on the way to creating lasting change. If you only have time for one thing, do the Action Step. If you have more time on your hands and want to take it a bit further, you can dive into the Further Thoughts section. These range from questions, journaling prompts, suggestions, and real-life examples, all designed to help you dig deeper and enhance your self-awareness.

1

COVERING THE BASICS

Just Three Things I Stopped Doing to Have a Happier Mind

I used to think that to "live better", have a happier mind, and move on from my past, I had to start doing five million new things. *I'll have to start juicing, jogging, meditating, doing headstands...* I thought to myself. The list is endless of things we feel we *should* start doing, right?

However, what I failed to realise for quite some time was that my new habits weren't really getting me where I wanted to go, and I couldn't figure out why. I had started the juicing, so why was I not feeling better? I had started doing my gratitude lists and putting all that positivity out there, so where was my Prince Charming? I had started meditating, so where was this promised peace of mind? And why was I still really quite miserable?

It took me a while to figure it out, but when I did, I realised it wasn't exactly rocket science. Things hadn't changed for me as much as I wanted them to simply because there were certain things I was still in the habit of doing daily, and they almost counteracted the new habits I was building.

So I started to look at some things I needed to stop doing, or things I needed to eliminate, and although I came up with a list of about five million (no exaggeration at all!), here are the most important three that I stopped doing to have a happier mind.

1. Blaming Others

In my teens and early twenties, I was a very angry person. I blamed everyone else for how I felt. For everything that didn't go the way I wanted it to, I had someone to blame: my parents, my friends, my teachers, my colleagues, my bosses... EVERY-ONE. Why? Because it was so much easier to blame others than to take responsibility for things myself. I blamed the guys I dated for my low self-esteem; I blamed other people for my low mood. Basically, if The Blame Game was an actual game, I would have won it over and over again.

I stopped participating in The Blame Game when I started seeing a psychiatrist in my twenties. I wasn't in a good place and was pretty exhausted from pretending that things were fabulous. Although this lady was brilliant, there was absolutely no beating around the bush with her. She did show me the empathy and care that I wanted, and she also gave me the kick up the backside I needed, which I am eternally grateful for. And when I finally woke up to the realisation that nothing was going to change until I changed, things started to improve. Properly facing up to that fact and accepting that other people can't actually be responsible for how I feel, or for my actions and behaviours (and not just reading it in some motivational quote page) was like finally getting the control I had been looking for.

The moral of the story? Stop blaming others. Take responsibility for your actions and behaviours because no one can drive you crazy unless you give them the keys.

What's just one thing you will do today to let go of that blame?

FURTHER THOUGHTS

- Is there anyone you currently blame?
- How does holding on to that blame help you?
- How would you benefit from removing that blame?

2. Chasing Perfection

Ah yes! The road to perfection: an isolated, critical, guilt-ridden, and frustration-filled journey. It sounds fantastic; where do I sign up?!

From a very young age I sought perfection. I wanted to be the perfect student, the perfect horse rider, the perfect daughter, the perfect friend, the perfect girlfriend, and I wanted to look perfect. And when it wasn't perfect I was a mess. The constant comparisons I created, the negative thought cycles that consumed my headspace, the mental battles, the lack of control, the constant dieting, the deflated self-esteem, the pain, the completely unrealistic expectations I had of myself and others, and all that for what? All in the pursuit of this thing I thought would make me happy: perfection.

And therein lies one of the many problems with chasing perfection: the story we tell ourselves about it. My story went like this: *When I get things perfect, or when I'm perfect, it means that I'm good enough. It means that I've got it right, which means I'm worthy, and then I'll be happy.* You can almost see the vicious cycle unfold before your eyes. By constantly chasing perfection I was chasing validation that I was good enough. But instead of stopping to validate myself, I was continually using external sources and measures to do so. *If I've lost weight, it means I've been successful this week. If I get that job, it means I'm good enough. If I get 100 percent in that exam, it means I'm smart. If he asks me out, it means I'm pretty enough.*

If it sounds like you're on the same road, do yourself a favour and turn around now because no good is going to come of it.

ACTION STEP

Start catching your own If... then... or When... then... thoughts and get yourself out of this thinking trap by challenging them. Ask yourself, *How helpful is this way of thinking? What is stopping me feeling good about myself right now?*

FURTHER THOUGHTS

• Where in your life do you aim for perfection?

3. Carrying Excess Baggage

With the new hand luggage restrictions on so many airlines nowadays, it's become even more important that we pack carefully and mindfully. And let's be honest, excess baggage is not only cumbersome but very expensive. I'm not giving actual luggage or packing advice here, but I am encouraging you to reflect on what you carry around with you every day.

Do you carry around Blame or Forgiveness? Guilt or Learnings? Hatred or Love? Anxiety or Acceptance? One choice will leave you free to travel light, whereas the other will always come at a price.

For years I carried around the uncomfortable feelings of blame and guilt, shame and anxiety. In fact, I rarely left home without them. And if I did happen to wake up in a good mood, I would actually make time to think about what I had to worry about or be angry about. I would literally ask myself, *Surely there's something not going right for me at the moment? What was that thing I was really pissed off about yesterday?* I remember even having to remind myself of something or someone I had to be annoyed with. What a great way to spend my time. I had no idea how heavy a burden all this "excess baggage" actually was, but I do know why I was still carrying it around—I felt I needed to constantly remind myself in order to protect myself from certain people who had hurt me before. The irony was that as much as I thought carrying all this stuff around was helping me, it was doing the complete opposite.

Bottom line? Carrying things from the past around with you only hinders you. It keeps you living in the past; it keeps you chained to the past. Carrying excess baggage daily takes its toll on your mental and physical health, so how about taking some time to do a little repacking today?

ACTION STEP

Explore the reasons why you might be holding on to your "excess baggage" by journalling or talking things over with a friend.

FURTHER THOUGHTS

- What excess baggage from the past are you carrying around?
- Some of us carry excess baggage because we think it protects us in some way; how does carrying this baggage help you?
- Who would you be if you didn't have to carry this baggage from the past with you?

Just Three Things I Started Doing to Make Life Easier for Myself

I t's amazing what happens when you take action to stop doing certain behaviours. Take carrying your past around with you as an example: I often think of this as like trying to move forward with one of those resistance bands around your waist. It's a constant struggle, yet some of us refuse to take the band off.

I found I had a lot more headspace and actual time when I got rid of my resistance bands—those bad habits that I did almost without noticing. And although stopping unhelpful behaviours is great, when it comes to creating change, it's not necessarily about stopping some habits or starting others, it's about running the two changes in parallel to get the best results. Sure, stopping smoking will improve my health, but when I couple that with getting more exercise, I'm going to create even better results for myself.

But deciding what to start focusing on can be confusing, and stressful in itself because of the plethora of "advice" and recommendations. I knew I had to start making life easier for myself, and the following three things helped me do just that.

1. Managing My Thoughts

Our thoughts are so powerful they control our feelings, actions, habits, and behaviours. If you want to produce a different set of results in your life, learning to manage your thoughts better is essential.

Although it's completely unrealistic to think we can control every single thought we have, what we're aiming to do here is manage the unhelpful, negative thoughts that like to hang around a little too long—like these:

Things never work out for me.
Everyone else is finding this so much easier than me.
What if I never meet anyone again?

Managing our thoughts starts with awareness. We've got to become aware of our own thought patterns and aware of the thinking traps we're prone to falling into, because without that awareness nothing changes.

When I discuss this aspect of mind-management with my clients, I often use the analogy of a hamster on a hamster wheel. We talk about slowing the hamster wheel of thoughts down and gaining control over it rather than allowing the thoughts to run riot and control us. Think about it: Negative thoughts don't usually hang out alone, so if you don't manage or deal with the first negative thought you catch, it can easily trigger another one, and another one... and before you know it, you're on the hamster wheel of negative thoughts and it's spinning at 100 miles an hour.

Although it can be the simplest of thoughts that sets our hamster wheel in motion, there are ten common thinking traps, or cognitive distortions, that are a surefire way to get pulled into that downward negative spiral. Below is a list of some of the most common thinking traps. Some of them might sound familiar, and you might even recognise them all as part of your own way of thinking, but just park the judgement for now.

Catastrophising: Blowing things out of proportion or making mountains out of molehills, as my mum would say. *Example: I can't believe I crashed the car; this is the worst day of my life.*

Double standards: Thinking it's okay for you to do something but not okay for someone else, or vice versa. *Example: It's okay for her to fail her driving test the first time around, but it's not okay for me.*

Mind reading: Imagining you know what someone is thinking. *Example: I know Billie is mad at me because she didn't say hello to me this morning.*

All-or-nothing/black-and-white thinking: Looking at the event in extreme terms and ignoring the shades of grey. *Example: There was nothing good about our holiday, absolutely nothing.*

Labelling: Judging people, or ourselves, based on a one-off behaviour. *Example: I locked my keys in the car; I'm so stupid,* or

She's pathetic; look at her throwing herself at that guy over there.

Unrealistic expectations: Placing a set of rules on ourselves or someone else and expecting them to be adhered to. Usually identified by *should, must,* and *have to. Example: I have to go to the gym every day,* or *He should know how I feel about this,* or *I must get everything right for this evening.*

Overgeneralising: Selecting one negative aspect of a situation and applying it across the board. *Example: I didn't get that job and so I'll never get a new one,* or *All men are...* or *All women are...* or *All lawyers are...* When we fall into this thinking trap, we might even expect the unwanted behaviour to happen again because we presume it's part of a pattern and not a one-off occurrence. *Example: She'll be late again. She was late the last time; she's always late.*

Personalisation: Thinking that things others say or do are a direct attack on us personally. *Example: When my husband Steve said his parents would love grandkids I know that was a dig at me.* Or it can also refer to comparisons we make between ourselves and others. *Example: Gina is in a bad mood. I must have done something to upset her.*

The reward fallacy: Believing that our good deeds and sacrifices have to pay off (notice the unrealistic expectation here) and getting frustrated when this doesn't happen. *Example: I'm a good person, so this shouldn't happen to me.*

Blaming: As it is! Blaming others for how we feel. *Example: She* *makes me feel really stupid and that's why I'm not participating in the session.*

I don't know about you, but when I read through that list, I just go tick, tick, tick beside each one as if it's a completed to-do list. Yes, I've done them all! When I think about the kinds of thought that used to race through my mind, I realise that my hamster wheel was spinning at 200 miles an hour. I had to get control of the wheel and slow that thing right down. I learned to do this by applying what I call the 3Cs: Catch, Challenge, and Change.

Step 1: Catch. Now that you know some of the most common thinking traps, you can catch them more easily. It does take time, but with awareness and practice it gets easier. It doesn't matter if you don't catch that initial triggering thought right away; that will come with time.

Step 2: Challenge. The best way to tackle thinking errors is to challenge their reliability. For example, imagine I start falling into the thinking trap of mind reading, thinking that my boss has asked to see me because she knows that I missed a deadline. I might then start to catastrophise, imagining myself getting fired, not being able to pay my bills, having to move home... I can stop that hamster wheel right there by asking myself, *How helpful is this thought right now?* Or, *Where's my evidence to support that thought?* It's not about ignoring what could go wrong, it's about checking the facts. Ask better questions and you'll get better answers. More on that in part 3 in this section.

Step 3: Change. We want to replace that negative thought with something more constructive. We're not talking about having happy, positive thoughts all the time because that's unrealistic. If I'm worried I might actually be fired and have good reason to believe it, ignoring the situation and thinking happy thoughts won't help me, but taking a deep breath and reminding myself that whatever happens I can deal with it, will. It's more constructive, it's resourceful, and it's empowering—and that's what we want.

I've been using the 3Cs for years now and it has made an enormous difference to the way I think about things. Of course, negative thoughts still pop up, but I'm able to catch them more quickly so they don't mushroom out of control. I'm a lot more in control of my thinking and as a result, more in control of my feelings, behaviours, actions, and habits. And we all know how good a bit more control feels, right?

ACTION STEP

Set yourself the goal of applying the 3Cs to one of your favourite common thinking traps over the next week.

FURTHER THOUGHTS

- What are some of your own most popular thinking errors?

2. Aiming for Your Version of Excellence

If you've read the previous sections, you'll already know how I feel about perfection and the problems it creates for people who chase after it. If you're aiming for perfection, the chances are that you will never be happy with the results you get; you'll be continuously frustrated with yourself and others because they usually won't live up to your unrealistic expectations either—brilliant!

However, when you aim for excellence rather than perfection, things change immediately, and for the better. Choosing excellence gives you more freedom because it removes the constraints that come with chasing perfection and allows room for growth.

Here's my reasoning behind ditching perfection for excellence: People who aim for excellence are usually more open to receiving and acting upon feedback because they're not blinkered and hindered by the one-track desire for perfection. And when you become more open to feedback, you can reflect on what you've done, make the relevant changes you want to make, and continue to progress. Aiming for excellence supports your personal and professional growth, not to mention your mental health.

So how do you know if you're on the right path? How do you know if you're aiming for excellence or just perfection in disguise? You've got to learn to draw the line—your own line. In aiming for excellence, the line that I use is *Am I doing my very best here?* If I can answer yes, then I know that's my line, I know that what I'm doing is good enough. Will it be good enough for someone else? Maybe not, but that's a different story.

Here's an example: I'm out to run my fastest marathon yet and I've set myself the goal of running it in 3:45 hours (at the time of writing this particular chapter, I'm training to beat this again!). My previous personal best was 3:52 hours, so I had some work to do. Now for some people, that time might seem slow and for others that might seem fast. For me, it meant busting my ass even more than I already had. So, on that Friday as I'm running the streets of Dubai, busting my ass, I wasn't even halfway around the course when I started feeling tired. My legs started to ache so badly, my heart was pounding so fast, and then that little thought—*This is hard, isn't it?*—popped up. That thought was quickly followed by, *You could just stop, you know, it's no one's race but your own... Go on, just pull over, you're so tired and you're only at the 17 km marker so it's not going to get any easier.* But knowing that slowing down or stopping wouldn't take me closer to my goal, I asked myself, *Am I really doing my best here? Really?* And my immediate answer was, *No, of course I'm not, I can do this.* And I pushed on.

However, with about 8 km left to go in the race, it was a different matter. I'd had to walk up a bridge, my calves were as tight as violin strings, my stomach ached, my quads were heavy, and I was really struggling. I stopped to stretch my calves, knowing that if I carried on the way I was going I risked not being able to finish the race at all. I looked at my watch; time was rapidly passing. At that stage I probably wasn't making my 3:45 goal. Tears welled up in my eyes. I started to beat myself up, which started the negative thought cycle (or hamster wheel) off again—great. But that wouldn't help me either, and knowing I needed to pull myself out of that thought cycle to get across that finish line, I asked myself again, *Am I really doing my best here? Is this me at my best?* And that time I could honestly say, *Yes! This is me doing my best and this is me at my best right now. I'm out here giving it everything I have, and regardless of how this race ends I'll be able to say I gave it everything.*

And that's good enough for me.

As it turned out, I finished my marathon in 3:47 hours, broken but absolutely elated with my effort.

For some people that wouldn't be good enough. For some people, the fact that I stopped to stretch my legs wouldn't be good enough either. But I'm not out to meet anyone else's standards when I run; I'm simply out to be the best I can be and that's how I know I'm aiming for excellence.

(ACTION STEP)

When you notice you're having unrealistic expectations of yourself, challenge those thoughts by asking, *Is this me at my very best here?* Once you can honestly say you're giving it your all, accept that as being good enough.

- What does it mean to you, to be at your best?
- How do you know when you're doing your best?
- Think about the times when you were really proud of yourself despite the end result. Can you find other areas in your life where this is true?

3. Learning to Love My Body

I'm a smart person and I was a very smart girl growing up, but I didn't always make very smart decisions. When I was about twelve, one of those not-smart decisions was that if I was thinner, I would be prettier and that would make me happier. I set out on a journey to get thinner and over time I became very good at it.

At thirteen, I knew the calorie content of every food. At fifteen, I started smoking because I heard and read that it was something people did to keep their weight down. During my very short experience as an apprentice jockey, I was even encouraged to smoke more. I became so self-conscious about how I looked that I weighed myself every morning and used that as a measure of my "success" and how I was "allowed" to feel: If I weighed less than yesterday, I could feel proud and happy with myself, but if I weighed more, I had no reason to be happy at all. Eating disorders are a slippery slope and I fell right in. By the age of twenty-one, I was diagnosed with anorexia, depression, and an anxiety disorder—my very own three things.

The journey to being comfortable with how I look and learning to love my body has been a long one, but one I am so glad to have embarked upon, because I would honestly hate to see where I'd be today if I hadn't. The journey started with getting professional medical help for my diagnosis, which involved therapy and medication, and although that made a difference, the real change began with managing my thoughts and changing my perception of my body. This is where running played a key role as it made me stronger mentally, physically, and emotionally. It helped me reframe my focus from being skinny to becoming stronger. I started to develop a better relationship with food, seeing it as fuel for my body instead of something to fear. I started to speak more kindly to my body, appreciating it and rewarding it for all it could do, instead of punishing it for what I had eaten. It's also amazing what you can focus on and accomplish when your headspace isn't consumed with the obsessive thoughts that an eating disorder brings. Had I still been caught in that cycle, I would never have the bandwidth to be such a fantastic wife, to pursue my dream career, and to write books!

Learn to love your body. After all, it's the only place you permanently live.

ACTION STEP

Write down three things that you appreciate about your body right now.

FURTHER THOUGHTS

- What's just one thing you can do this week to show your body that you appreciate it?
- What made you feel beautiful this week?
- What has your body helped you achieve this week?

Just Three Things I Continue to Work On

'How long will it take, Linda?'
I often get asked this by my coaching clients when they're considering investing in coaching for themselves. Now, although I can always give my clients an approximate timeframe for the work we'll do together, I also encourage them to remember that when it comes to their personal growth and development, there is no end date. The one thing in life that's certain is change, and we're all works in progress—myself included.

When it came to writing this chapter, I was sure I had my just three things for it. I started writing a first piece on patience because patience is definitely something I continue to work on (ask my husband!), but as soon as I started writing it, it didn't feel right at all. Delete, delete, delete. That's not to say that patience isn't important to me and something I can simply ignore, but for me, it was a safe option. If I spoke about how I continue to work on developing patience, I wouldn't have to admit or discuss some of the areas where I still struggle. I wrote a piece on asking for help. Delete, delete, delete. Again, that's not to say that asking for help isn't something I still work on; it is, but again, it was a safer option. By playing it safe I was keeping myself safe too—safe from the judgement of others. After all, who wants to be judged? Who would volunteer for that? But if I'm to show up as my authentic self and if that's what I try to empower my clients to do too, then it was time to allow myself to really be seen.

I was stuck, so I went out for a run, hoping to find some inspiration along the way. I was trying to figure out what I really and truly needed to write about in this section, even if it was hard to admit to. What do I need to own up to? What's something I continue to work on? What's something I catch myself doing, feel awful for doing it, and remind myself to continue working on it? *Well, we have a long list here, Linda!* shouts my inner critic.

1. Judging Others

I remember sitting at a formal event a few years ago, in a very ostentatious and beautiful hotel. As a guest, I had been reminded of the mandatory dress code for the evening. I was sitting with some friends, looking around, waiting for the event to begin, when I noticed a lady sitting in the next aisle wearing flip-flops with a skirt and t-shirt. I nudged my neighbour to get her attention. 'Oh my God,' she said. 'She's got to be the guest of some VIP to rock up dressed like that!' I said.

The event got underway, all was going smoothly, and soon

it was time for the guest speaker. I was excited to hear this lady. I didn't know a lot about her, but from her bio in the program, she sounded unbelievably inspiring. She was constantly working to raise awareness and money for her own charity that built homes and schools for children. Her recent achievements included completing seven marathons on seven continents and she was preparing to summit Everest. What a woman. The compere called the guest speaker to the stage and as the audience applauded, I couldn't believe who stood up to make her way to the podium—I was mortified. The woman whom I had thought wasn't dressed appropriately for the event was the guest speaker. I slid down in my seat, completely ashamed of my judgements as this lady told the audience her story of coming from nothing. Finishing high school, paying for her own education, and recognizing that she had so much more than other people, she sold all her possessions and began dedicating her money and life to helping others. I was consumed by my own guilt and horrified at how I had judged this lady based on her appearance.

So I do my best now to be mindful of the lessons I've learned through interactions like that, and I'm more careful to recognise judgements I'm making and park them. I certainly don't get it right all the time, but we're all works in progress, right?

And I do know that when I work to park those judgements, I'm creating a stronger foundation for building better relationships.

ACTION STEP

The next time you notice you're judging something about someone else, get curious about that judgement. Ask yourself, *I wonder what I can learn about myself here?* Self-awareness is powerful.

FURTHER THOUGHTS

- We often judge things in others that we don't want to face about ourselves. How true is this for you?
- When are you most likely to judge others?
- What's a powerful reminder you could use to help you move out of a place of judgement?

2. Managing My Expectations

I should be able to get all of this done, what is wrong with me?

What was he thinking? I've told him a thousand times already I don't eat red meat!

My coach should know I wouldn't be happy with that result. Does she know me at all?

My expectations are often as high as the Empire State Building on top of Burj Khalifa and as unrealistic as me making the US Olympic Figure Skating team—I can't even skate! But does that stop me from having the expectations? No, where's the fun in that?! There is none, but where there's high expectations you can bet your bottom dollar there's plenty of frustration too, and that's no fun either. Managing my expectations of myself and of others is something I continually work on, and trust me when I say I'm a massive project under construction with this one!

In an ideal world, people would know what we mean the first time we tell them, and it would remain at the forefront of their brain whenever they communicate with us after that. But that's not the reality at all. If we want someone to remember something about us, it's our job to communicate that with the person/people in question. Just because something is important to us, does not mean it's important to everyone else.

When I started dating my husband, I told him I didn't eat red meat. I definitely told him. I remember the situation distinctly: We were out for dinner and I told him I didn't eat red meat. I then presumed—that magic word—that because he liked me and wanted to see me again, he'd remember that fact about me in the same way that I'd remember he loves pizza and basically everything pizza-based. A few dates later, he very kindly offered to cook me dinner. He was getting everything ready in the kitchen and was very excited about the 'amazing beef' he was able to get in the local supermarket. 'And it's even Irish, for you,' he said. It was early days in our relationship, I really liked him, but inside I was already thinking, *A few weeks of dating and he's not listening to me already—ridiculous! What part of I don't eat red meat does he not get? We had a full conversation about it!* Then, thankfully, the rational part of me jumped in with, *Maybe he forgot? You've forgotten things about people you care about before, remember? It's nice of him to cook for you and he's proud of the fact it's something Irish too. Just tell him again.*

And I did tell him. And we laughed about it. And he was delighted to get to eat my portion of the meat. Winner-winner, veggie dinner!

ACTION STEP

Unrealistic expectations of ourselves and others are often marked in our language by words such as *should, need to, have to,* and *must.* Catch yourself the next time you use these words and check out the expectation behind them, asking yourself if it's realistic or not.

FURTHER THOUGHTS

Our expectations of others are a reflection of our own beliefs. But because our beliefs don't always help us and can in fact limit us, it's important that we become aware of these too. As you check out the expectations you have of others, explore the beliefs behind those expectations. *Example:* If I expect Steve to spend a fortune on me for my birthday because I believe that's how you show love to someone, that's a pretty limiting belief to hold. Can you imagine the frustration that would trigger in me?

3. Asking Myself, What Do People Experience When They Experience Me?

'Are you f**king serious? I'm walking here; you've a red light! What a d*ck!'

'Damn right I'm serious, lady, f**k you!'

And despite the fact that I had the right of way on the street that day, the fact that I reacted in such a manner bothered me for hours afterward. *Was I rude to him? Could he even give a rat's ass? Did other people think I was rude?*

I sat across from a lady I greatly admire one day and she asked me, 'Linda, what do people experience when they experience you?' The question literally threw me back in my chair and I was speechless. In that second, my day so far flashed before my eyes. I saw the way I had treated someone on my way to that very meeting, and I wasn't happy with myself. Since that day and almost on a daily basis, I ask myself that same question: *What do people experience when they experience me?* And as if by habit now, it pops into my head like a reminder, like a checkpoint: *How am I interacting with this person right here, right now?*

I continue to ask myself this question for a number of reasons. One, it reminds me to be kind. It costs absolutely nothing to be nice and I do believe the world could always benefit from a little more kindness, even if it's just a smile. Two, I believe that it's important to be congruent—to practice what I preach. If I would like my clients, and indeed people in general, to step back, reflect, and make positive changes in how they interact with others, a good starting point is modelling that behavior myself. Three, it keeps me on my toes as a businesswoman. Here's why: Your reputation is what people say about you when your back is turned or when you leave the room, not while you're in it, and people will always talk about how they experienced you; how you made them feel. As Maya Angelou said, "I've learned that people will forget what you said, people will forget what you did, but people will never forget how you made them feel".

People will remember their experience of you and with you. If my purpose is to inspire, to motivate, to encourage, and to empower people to create the change they want to see in their lives, then that's the experience I want people to have when they are in my company. That's what I want people to experience when they experience me.

ACTION STEP

Complete your own personal 360 feedback review. Choose five people in your life and write down what you think they experience when they experience you. To challenge yourself more with this, make sure at least two of those people are not within your close circle of friends.

FURTHER THOUGHTS

- What do people who don't know you very well experience when they experience you? *Example:* I'm more reserved around people I don't know or people I'm not comfortable with. That can make me come across as uninterested or even rude at times.

- What do people experience when you're stressed/worried/anxious?
- What could people experience when you're at your best?

Just Three Things to Get Your Day Off to a Better Start

U p until my early thirties, I used to wake up to the immediate thought of, *SH*T! I've to go to work*, and immediately I'd start listing all the things I had to do when I got to work. Then when I was done listing those, I'd begin listing all the things I had to do after work. Naturally, there'd be quite a few complaints thrown in there for good measure: I don't have enough time, I don't have enough money, I don't have enough space, I don't have any clothes to wear, I don't have, I don't have, I don't have. And then I'd wonder why I didn't have a great day. Really?

That pattern continued until I did my first coaching course; that same repetitive pattern of negativity until I properly examined how I was starting each day. I had never thought of it before and when I was asked the question, 'What's the first thing you think of when you wake up in the morning?' I was ashamed at the realisation that despite everything I have in life, despite everything I've been blessed with, my initial thought was, *Sh#T! I've to go to work!* And that was the first thing that I changed... The others followed.

Here are just three things anyone can do to get their day off to a better start.

1. Practice Gratitude

The more I read about personal growth, success, and happiness, the more this whole "gratitude practice" kept popping up; it was everywhere. As a result, I began making two little words, 'thank you', not just the first words I utter in the morning but also the first thoughts I have.

What does it mean to actually practice gratitude? For me, practicing something is about action. Walking around in the morning saying thank you is great—as long as it's intentional and not just a "tick box" exercise.

Here's where I encourage you to go one step further and write down what you're grateful for. It's great when gratitude is in our heads and hearts; it's even more powerful when we take action and write it down. There's very interesting evidence behind the power of writing something out by hand: It can create a stronger sense of closeness to what we're writing about, it can help us slow down, to notice other aspects of what we're writing about that we may not have noticed had we just kept those thoughts in our head. You don't have to write a whole novel before you have your first cup of coffee, but how about starting with a list of what you're thankful for in that very moment, even if it's a list of just three things?

As much as I love gratitude lists, at one stage I noticed that I was falling into a habit trap of listing some of the same things each morning. For example: I'm grateful for having Steve in my life, for my career, for having the legs to run, blah, blah, blah. It was like my gratitude practice had become that "tick box" task, which defeats the whole purpose. Sure, there's nothing wrong with having the same things on your gratitude lists—having the legs to run will always be on mine!—but I noticed I had become less mindful about my practice. Interestingly enough, when I fall into that habit of rattling off the usual items, I often get the feeling that it's not working—that the gratitude practice isn't having the same effect on me as it has had on all those successful people. That's my cue to do something different. Now, when I recognise I'm falling into that habit, I consider using the acronym NOP—Nature, Opportunities, and People—to help direct my focus and create variety in my gratitude practice. I ask myself, *What specifically about nature am I grateful for?* Or, *What in the greater aspect of the world am I grateful for? What opportunities am I grateful for today? Who in my life am I grateful for right now? What is it about those people that I'm grateful for?* These kinds of question also help me look at the details or the specifics of something more. Saying I'm grateful for my best friend, Aideen, is great, and recognising that I'm especially grateful for her logical advice in making that decision the other day is even better. Get into the details of your gratitude whenever you can. What difference does this person make to your life? What difference does that thing make to your day?

And finally, I've noticed that the days when I tell myself I don't have time to write things down or the days when my headspace is filled with complaints, self-doubt, or self-pity are the days I need the practice even more.

ACTION STEP

Bearing NOP in mind, write down just three things you're grateful for when you first wake up tomorrow morning.

FURTHER THOUGHTS

- Get into the details of your gratitude whenever you can. If you're grateful for someone in your life, what difference, specifically, does that person make to your life?
- What difference does that thing in nature make to your day?
- What made that opportunity you identified so valuable?

2. Learn Something

I've always been a voracious reader, but when I was teaching full-time I found that I spent so much of my time either reading history books or students' essays that I didn't read for pleasure as much as I used to, and I missed it. I read a lot of running books when I started running more, but I wasn't satisfying that craving for learning I had. I thought about what I could change in order to create more time to read, tried a few things, and then the obvious change was to get up earlier.

So that's what I started doing. I set the alarm clock for fifteen minutes earlier than I was used to getting up, and I noticed the more I did that, the more I came to value this time. Not only did it give me the peaceful start to the day that I loved, but I always felt accomplished after it too. I'd get my cozy dressing gown on and curl up on the sofa while it was still dark outside and read with a purpose to learn, be it learning new facts, a new coaching technique, or a new perspective on something.

When you make that time to learn something in the morning it's a fantastic feeling, and when you can share what you've learned with someone else during the day it's even better. I deliberately stayed away from reading the news, not because I wanted to be ignorant but because rarely was there anything on the news feeds that made me smile or brightened up my morning.

ACTION STEP

Set yourself the goal of finding a book that's interesting enough to be worth setting your alarm clock a little earlier!

FURTHER THOUGHTS

- What are you learning about yourself as you read this book? *Example:* One of the many things I learned about myself as I wrote it was that chunking bigger projects into smaller tasks always makes the work more manageable.
- Where else can you start to apply those learnings?
- What's just one thing you'd love to learn but you've never gotten around to? *Example:* I've always wanted to learn Italian and although I'll listen to language

podcasts during the day, I've often used my time in the morning to learn a few new words in relation to the topic I'm currently learning about.

3. Ask Yourself What Needs to Be Different Today

You can't have a good day today if you keep thinking about what a bad day you had yesterday. So use the morning as an opportunity (if you haven't done so already the night before) to ask yourself what needs to be done differently today. The following questions or journal prompts are ones that I use regularly and will help you too. Keep in mind that this will work even better if you can carve out a few minutes to write down your answer instead of keeping it in your head. Perhaps you could work on them right after your gratitude list?

What needs to be done differently today?
For me, today needs to be different in terms of how I spend my time. Yesterday, I spent too much time flapping around from one thing to another and not getting anything done. So today, I need to sit down and do one task at a time. Even if I get the urge to step away from that task, I know that staying focused serves me better.

What am I prioritising today?
Today, I'm prioritising my next literature review for my Positive

Psychology course. This means getting my word count down to 2500, instead of the 4,000 it's currently at. This also means that I don't open any emails or answer any enquires about my new app Upstrive until I've got my word count down.

What am I doing today that helps me now and in the future?
Focusing on my literature review today helps me meet the goal of getting my assessment ready for submission next week, but it also helps me gather data for all the work I'm doing for Upstrive now and in the future too. Going for a run today also helps manage my stress today and helps my training overall.

ACTION STEP

Wanting to do today differently often involves having to prioritise differently. Use the following Urgent/Important table to help you do just that:

	URGENT	NOT URGENT
IMPORTANT	**1. Necessity/Do First (high importance & high urgency)** Literature review for Positive Psychology course	**2. Less Urgent/Plan/Quality/ Decide (high importance & not urgent)** Emails Reply to enquiries about Upstrive
NOT IMPORTANT	**3. Delegate or Delay (not important but urgent; usually for someone else)** Going for a run—I don't have to go this morning, I can go this evening.	**4. Delete (not urgent and not important)** Social media—it's just not happening today and that's fine.

FURTHER THOUGHTS

- Keep an eye on how often you answer the question *What needs to be different today?* with yet more things for your to-do list. Sometimes it's not about creating more things to do, it's about recognising how you spend the time that you have. How many times a day do you find yourself saying or thinking, *I don't have time for that or I'm too busy?*

- I get that we're busy, I get that there are hundreds of demands on us, but if we're too busy to look after our own priorities, there's something wrong. *Example:* Being a part of my nieces' and nephews' lives is really important to me, but if I never have time to spend with them when I'm at home because I still schedule client calls, what does that say about my priorities?

Just Three Ways to Deal with Your Past

I work with people on a daily basis who are usually fighting something in their past.

And I can fully empathise with what it's like to do that because I'm also one of those people. Although I understand that we often keep the fight going as a way of protecting ourselves from being hurt like we have been before, I also know how unhelpful it is—trust me, I'm an expert in this area!

One of the good things about our past is that that's where it is; it's gone, it's done, and it can only keep coming back controlling or influencing the present if we allow it to. The other thing to remember about our past is that even though it's done, it's still a part of us. So, yes, although we all have things in our past that we're not proud of, there's no getting away from the fact that our past is part of us. The best thing about all of this is that we're always in full control of how we deal with it. We can choose to let unwanted aspects of it come back and dictate how we think, feel, and behave, or we can take control of it. The choice is always yours—choose wisely. Just keep in mind that if you don't learn to deal with your past, it's going to keep showing up in your present.

1. Accept It

Hands up if you've ever spent time wishing, wanting, and hoping the past could be different.

Keep your hands up if you know that's not constructive at all.

And keep your hands up if you still do it anyway!

One way to deal with your past is to accept ownership of it. In accepting what happened, you're already in a better position to deal with it and move forward because it's incredibly empowering to own and accept all the parts of ourselves, not just the ones we like. A first step you can take is to accept your past for what it was, resisting the urge to criticise, judge, or blame. Accept what happened. It's done.

Accept that you cannot change it. Accept that whatever happened, you made the best choice at the time with the resources available to you. Perhaps at the time you didn't have the patience, wisdom, courage, understanding, or any other resource that you needed to produce a different result, or perhaps you know differently now than you did back then. When we look back at our past, we often do so through the unrealistic lens of hindsight, which can cause us to criticise ourselves for our "poor choices", or label ourselves as "stupid" for not knowing better, but the reality is that we don't know what we don't know and we can't use what we don't have access to.

I was quick to criticise myself for not being more assertive in certain situations when I was younger, but I was also quick to forget that I didn't have the confidence or the skills I would have needed at that time to be more assertive. Beating yourself up over what happened and telling yourself you *should* have known better is never going to help you move forward and only keeps you chained to the past.

Accept that you are not your past. You're not a period in your history, you don't live there anymore, and therefore there's no reason to judge yourself on something that happened back then.

Accept, accept, accept.

Practice self-compassion instead of looking at your past through hindsight and berating yourself for what you did. How? Accept that you did the best you could at that time with what you knew and what you had. *Example:* I could easily sit around and berate myself for allowing my eating disorder and depression to ruin so much of my adolescence and twenties, but how does that help me? Part of the process of accepting what happened involved realising that I was just doing my best in difficult circumstances, and I was finding whatever ways of coping I could think of.

FURTHER THOUGHTS

- How does berating yourself for your past mistakes help you?

- What would you need in order to be able to accept your past fully and completely?
- How much of what you need is actually within your control?

2. Reframe It

Have you ever dealt with something by sweeping it under the carpet, doing your best to forget about it, and just kind of hoping that it would stay there, never to resurface? How did that work out for you? Because I failed miserably when I tried it!

When it comes to dealing with our past, we always have a choice: We can continue to sweep things under the carpet, ignoring and pretending they don't exist, or we can deal with it. And although dealing with it is the harder thing to do and we love things that are easy, it serves us better in the long run.

When you look at past events that hurt you, or past mistakes that you've made, instead of dwelling on the negative details of those events, reframe what you see by looking for the lessons you learned and the resources you gained from the experience. When you choose to reframe situations, you're empowering yourself in a number of ways, equipping yourself with additional tools in your toolkit, and reminding yourself of the lessons you've learned, and we all know that knowledge is power.

If I ever start to feel sorry for myself about past relationships, instead of starting down the road of criticising myself for not knowing better and not doing something different, I stop and remind myself of the biggest gains from those experiences, such as having respect for myself, establishing stronger boundaries, and paying attention to people's behaviour as a form of communication and not just their words. How could you argue with having more respect for yourself? How empowering.

I apply this technique to work situations that didn't always go my way: Instead of shirking away from the situation and pretending it didn't happen, I recognise it and reframe it as a lesson in courage, humility, communication, and openness, and that allows me to shrug it off. When we reframe in a way that works for us, we no longer feel the need to sweep things under the carpet.

We all make mistakes; we're only human. But we're also often our own worst enemies as some of us feel the need to repeatedly punish ourselves for our past mistakes, making sure we can still feel the pain, the suffering, the guilt, the shame, and, of course, the blame. Let's not forget the blame. The problem is that if you continually carry around the past with you, you're never fully living in the present—how can you?

Something can be learned from every situation, but with some situations we have to look a little more closely to find the lesson.

ACTION STEP

Many of us play the victim role in the story we tell ourselves about the past, but how would it be if we played the role of the champion or protagonist instead? Set aside fifteen to

twenty minutes and apply this new role to a problem from
your past that still affects you.

- What did you learn about yourself through the
  experience?
- What did you learn about others through the
  experience?
- How does the champion within you view this experience now?

3. Change the Way You See It

When it comes to dealing with our past, the lens we choose
to view it through matters. It matters a lot.

When we change the way we've coded or stored a particular experience, we change the meaning we've placed on the
experience and therefore how we feel about it.

For example, imagine there's a conversation I had with
someone that I'm still really embarrassed about. It's not something that causes me great anguish, but I'd feel a lot better if
I could have a different reaction when the memory shows up
in my mind. When I think of that conversation, I notice these
three things first:

1. I'm in it and seeing everything through my own eyes;
   I'm fully immersed in the experience instead of being
   an observer.

2. The memory shows up as a movie scene.
3. It's really brightly coloured and I see lots of details in it.

Because these three aspects of the memory are most obvious for me, adjusting them changes how I will experience the memory as I move forward.

1. Instead of being in the memory, I'll take myself out of the scene, as if I'm watching myself like an observer.
2. I'll turn the movie scene into a snapshot so there's no longer any movement.
3. I'll imagine the snapshot in black and white, or even drain it entirely of colour so all I have left is a blank photo that looks like it never developed properly.

Here's what I experienced when I made those three changes to the memory of that conversation.

1. When I took myself out of the memory and imagined I was just an observer, I immediately noticed I wasn't as embarrassed about the situation. I find making this change alone can be extremely helpful in reducing emotional attachment to memories—for myself and my clients.
2. When I turned the movie scene into a snapshot, the memory instantly lost a lot of significance because I had placed so much meaning on the other person's reaction. Without the movement involved in the person's reaction, the meaning wasn't there anymore.
3. I'm a highly visual person and pay a lot of attention

to details, so when I played around with the colour in this image I noticed that when I turned it black and white, it seemed too old to be real. When I faded it to a near-white image, I could no longer see any details, so the image no longer impacted me the way it used to.

ACTION STEP

Why not give it a go yourself?

Choose a past experience you'd like to feel differently about. To start, I recommend choosing an experience that's not particularly heavy for you; think of something that might be a three or a four on an emotional scale of one to ten. When you think of that experience, what are some of the things you immediately notice? Write those down.

Once you've got a list of your submodalities or components of the image, you can work on changing them one by one and noticing the difference it makes to how you feel about it. Sometimes when we change one component, it can automatically affect another part. For example, when I took a client through this exercise, as soon as they disassociated themselves from the image and became an observer, they said the image immediately became smaller and moved farther away. It might also help to imagine that you have a remote control for changing aspects of the image or a dimmer switch to drain colour. I've found this works really well with my younger clients, so for any of you with children, encourage them to try this technique for themselves.

Give it a go and find out what works best for you. As my fabulous NLP (Neuro-Linguistic Programming) trainers say, 'It's like throwing spaghetti at the wall and seeing what sticks!'

FURTHER THOUGHTS

+ Pay attention to the size of the memory; how does making the image bigger or smaller affect how you feel about it?
+ If there's sound associated with the memory, play around with the sounds and notice the difference that makes. What happens when you switch the sound off? What difference does changing a voice in the memory make? If you're annoyed by something your boss said, imagine what they'd sound like if they were Daffy Duck. How does a change like that affect how you feel?
+ If there's music associated with the memory that bothers you, try out a few different soundtracks to see what difference they make. Playing circus music or something silly can help us laugh at ourselves or reduce the serious tone we had applied to the situation.

Just Three Changes to Make to Your Language

H ow would it be if we were to choose our words as carefully as we choose other things that are important to
us? We might place importance on being on time for
someone but not be mindful of the words we use when we're
in their company. We might spend considerable time choosing
an outfit for an occasion but not consider the impact of our
own negative self-talk. We might place value on saving money
and criticise others unintentionally for what they *should* do
with theirs.

As soon as I started learning about NLP I became even more
aware of how powerful our words are, how they literally have
the ability to make or break a situation, or even a relationship.
And when I started training to become an NLP coach, I saw
the evidence of this very quickly. I noticed how often I told
myself I *should* do something and then wondered why I felt so
demotivated or guilty. I saw my students show more interest
in receiving feedback when they realised there was no *but*
coming after initial positive statements.

As always, it's about making small changes to create bigger and better results in your life. Making changes to the language you use is no different.

1. Do Something about *But*

'Well, the chicken is nice...'

'I know it's not your fault you were held up at the meeting...'

'It's a nice idea...'

I don't know what pops into your head when you read or hear those statements. What I hear is *but, but, but...*

And what happens as soon as we hear that *but*? Yup, we usually ignore the positive statement that preceded it and choose to hang on to the negative instead, because *but* negates anything positive that came before it. That compliment we were "trying" to give has become as useful as a chocolate teapot.

First, I don't want any complaints about how many times I've used *but* in this book so far—my book = my rules! Second, I'm not saying that we get rid of *but* completely. I am saying that we need to do something about it. Because it doesn't matter who you're communicating with, when you bring *but* into the conversation, it removes that positive intention to compliment, and it can create ambiguity and encourage defensiveness.

'I'm sorry I lied to you, but you're so sensitive about these things.' *Well, there's one way to make a disaster out of an "apology".*

'It's a great idea, but I don't see it working.' *But(!) if you think it's a great idea, can't we talk about how it could potentially work? What am I missing here?*

'Great talk, Linda, but I didn't know where you were going with it.' *Was it a great talk or not?*

So, what can we do about *but*? One thing we can do is remove it altogether.

'I'm sorry I lied to you, I was trying to protect you. I know now that didn't work well.'

'It's a great idea, I'm just unsure if it will work.'

'Great talk. Linda. What are you hoping people will really take away from it?'

Another thing we could do is replace *but* with *and*.

'I like you and I need my own space too.'

'I'm sorry I upset you and I'll do my best to be more aware of how you're feeling.'

The power of using *and* instead of *but* is such a simple change AND it encourages more win-win situations. This isn't about sugarcoating the message you need to be conveyed; it's about influential communication, which means getting the best from everyone involved and for everyone involved.

Catch yourself when you go to use *but* and become aware of your purpose in doing so. Could *and* be more helpful? Notice how it feels when others use *but* with you. What thoughts does it trigger?

FURTHER THOUGHTS

* Sometimes we use *but* as an excuse or a way out of something. How true is this for you?
* Catch yourself next time you use *but* as an excuse and think about what you really wanted to say instead... but you didn't!
* What encourages you to use excuses in the situations where you do? More often than not it's because we don't want to hurt the other person's feelings. Fear can play a powerful role too. *Example:* We've no interest in going to the art exhibition with our friend because we think it's boring, but we might be afraid to admit that.

2. Stop *Should*-ing All Over Yourself

Every time I hear this word, alarm bells go off in my head; it's like nails down a chalkboard to me.

Should implies a certain level of expectation, and not always realistic expectation. It has that commanding or authoritative sound to it, like it's tied to a rule or set of rules that have been set—quite often by someone else—and I'm sure we all know what happens when we don't obey that command or those rules. Ah yes, let's open the door and invite guilt and shame in, fantastic! Why not bring blame in too, and then we'll have the full set?

I should have been able to get here on time.
Really? Even with that traffic accident, not to mention the fact that the car wouldn't start and your children needed some help getting ready? You still *should* have been able to get there on time? Where's the flexibility? Where's the choice here? I'm not saying that we allow ourselves to become lax about punctuality or our commitments, but (yes, there it is again!) there really has to be some wiggle room. Things don't always go according to plan—as I'm sure we all know—and the person with the greatest flexibility will always have the greatest choice. If you ask me, *should* removes choice and that's not always a good thing.

I should go to the gym now.
Sometimes we even use the word in an attempt to motivate ourselves, but how motivating is it really? You *should* go to the gym? Says who? I am fully aware that different words work as motivators for different people, and if you think *should* is your motivating word, then fine, go for it. Personally, I don't see it as motivating at all ,and most of my clients are far more motivated by kinder words than *should*. If you're using *should* as a motivating word and you're still not motivated, that's an indication something needs to change. Do yourself a favour today and begin to replace *should* with words that work better for you. Why not

go with, I *will* make every effort to be there on time, or, I'm *going* to the gym now, and see how they feel for you?

You should have known better.
And there's the finger of blame that seems to extend automatically when we use this word in certain contexts with other people—or even with ourselves. *You should have known better.* I feel patronised. I feel I've done something wrong that I had the opportunity to do differently. I feel guilty. I feel I've let someone down and disappointed them. I feel shame. I think we could all agree that none of these are comfortable feelings, so let's stop *should*-ing all over ourselves and others and leave *should* where it belongs—in the dictionary.

We've seen how guilt-inducing *should* can be, so the next time it shows up, consider being kinder to yourself. Give yourself a break and do something nice for youself instead of beating yourself with that guilt stick.

FURTHER THOUGHTS

- When *should* shows up, get curious about where it's coming from; after all, it's not always our own voice that whispers or shouts it. Where does your *should* come from?

- Knowing that *should* often represents a rule or a set of rules, when it shows up, get curious about who owns those rules—where have they come from?
- Instead of a swear jar, get yourself a should jar and make a financial donation to it every time you mention the s-word, or even think it!

3. Replace *Try* with *Will/Do*

I have a confession to make: I was still a high school history teacher when I completed my first NLP course and my students were my guinea pigs. I was practicing all the little language nuances I had learned on them, and boy what a difference it made to both the way I interacted with my students and the results I got from them.

One of the first changes I made was I stopped asking my students to *try* their best and reminded them to *do* their best. I was so surprised that such a simple change brought about such a big difference in their work ethic. I noticed that when I said something like, 'Try question two' my students took it to mean there was an option, there was a choice or a get-out clause, and although I'm all for choice, when it came to exam-style questions in my classroom... there was no choice! So, I dropped the *try* and started saying, 'Do question two once you've finished question one' and as a result, their willingness to get on task was quicker and their ability to consider new and better ways of accomplishing their tasks improved.

My problem with *try* is that there's just no commitment;

it's shrouded in doubt. Even the command itself offers a choice of action or not. 'Try doing that one again and see how you go' is almost like you could take it or leave it. There's no definite action. And if my students wanted to do well, they had to take action.

It's the same in a coaching context when I hear a client say, 'I'll try and get my tasks done'. The alarm bells go off in my head and my immediate response is, 'What would you need to just do the tasks?' Even a simple 'I'll do my best' sounds like it has more drive and purpose than 'I'll try my best', and that's what we want. We want action to be taken so change can be created and progress made.

For some people it's simply a figure of speech or a natural polite response to a request, but test out these *try* sentences for yourself and notice your immediate reaction to them.

I'll try and be there.
I'll try and implement some of the tips from this book.
I'm trying to give up smoking.

With the first, I'm presuming the person won't show up at all (although maybe that says more about me than it does about them!) With the second and third, it makes me think the person isn't really serious about change. They sound a bit blasé; there's no commitment.

What do you do instead? I've had numerous conversations with clients where they tell me they only tell someone they'll *try* and do something because they don't want to let them down. Of course, I see the positive intention, but how do you think they'll feel when you don't follow through on your words?

There are other ways of showing that positive intention without saying you'll *try*.

I want to support you with this, I've just got a lot going on right now.
I won't be able to make it, how can I make it up to you?
I won't make it by nine p.m., it will be nine-thirty at the earliest.

ACTION STEP

Either seek to do your best to honour a commitment or don't commit to it. If you're serious about something, make sure the language you use reinforces that. There's nothing wrong with giving yourself wiggle room, just be honest.

FURTHER THOUGHTS

- The next time you hear yourself saying, 'I'll try', ask yourself, *Is this something I really want to do?*
- If it is something you want to do, ask yourself, *What would I need to just commit to it?*
- Of course, if it's not something you want to do, what stops you from just saying so?

Just Three Things to Keep in Mind When Goal Setting

O ne of the things I absolutely love about my job as a coach is seeing transformation take place in my clients' lives. I love working with them to set meaningful and often challenging goals and then see them go out and smash it—it's incredible. I've seen my clients create transformation in so many different areas of their lives, from getting their dream job to becoming their own boss, from leaving a relationship that no longer empowered them to meeting their ideal partner. Regardless of the transformation my clients created, it all started with setting clear and compelling goals.

Setting goals is such a powerful process in so many ways: It helps us direct our focus to what we want, instead of focusing on what we don't want; it gives us clarity on where we're going so we can measure our progress enroute; and it encourages us to be more solution-focused in our thinking and action-orientated in our procedure.

Goal setting has made a massive difference to my own life in helping me create the changes I wanted. When I was younger,

I always had an idea of what I wanted but rarely made the time to get clear on what that really meant or how I could even go about getting it. It was only when I experienced coaching myself that I realised why I had been floundering around for so long. Use this section to help you create the clarity you need and set yourself those goals that you've been putting off.

1. Set a Clear Outcome

Don't think of a pink elephant. I mean it. Whatever you do, do not think of that pink elephant. And of course what are you thinking of? A pink elephant.

What I often find with my coaching clients (and myself) is that we can be very good at knowing what we don't want and not always that great at knowing what we do want. The first step in goal setting is setting yourself a clear outcome that is built around what you want. Let me use an example from a coaching conversation with one of my clients.

I've known my client, Tom, for a while now. Tom will usually give me a call when something pops up in his life that he could use some direction with.

Me: Right, let's get started. What's our focus for today's session?

Tom: I've been thinking that I'm kinda over dating random girls and would really like a relationship at this stage.

Me: Okay, what kind of a relationship?

Tom: Oh, you know, the usual.

Me: I don't know. What's "the usual"?

Tom: You know, like one that people have usually.

Me: We have a relationship. Is this what you mean?

Tom: Oh God, no!

Me: [laughing]

Tom: No, seriously, Linda... I want a relationship with someone I can hang out with.

Me: Good, now we're getting somewhere. What else? Is it just about hanging out with someone? Like a work colleague? Or one of your football mates?

Tom: No, not like one of the lads. I want a romantic relationship. I want to see myself with someone long-term.

Me: What does that look like for you?

Obviously I had an idea of the type of relationship Tom was talking about, but I couldn't just presume that we were on the same wavelength. *Relationship* means different things to different people. You have get very specific about what it is that you actually want.

(ACTION STEP)

Choose an area of your life that you'd like to create change in. What does that change look like, specifically, for you?

FURTHER THOUGHTS

◆ How will you know when you've achieved this goal?

> *Example:* Think about what will be different. If you're setting a financial goal around saving, is it about seeing X amount of money in the bank?
> ◆ What's the importance to you of achieving this goal? *Example:* Some people save money for a sense of security, to have their own house, to travel, etc.
> ◆ How will you measure your progress? *Example:* Consider milestones that you can build in along the way that will help you reflect on what's working or what you might need to change.

2. Set SMARTER Goals

Although SMART goals are good, SMARTER goals are better. Use the following to upgrade your goals and make them even more compelling.

Simple: Keep your goal stated in simple language. Make it too complex and you invite room for ambiguity. How simple is your current goal?

Maintainable (by you): If you can't take action yourself or you're relying on external factors to achieve your goal, it's less likely you'll accomplish it. How easy is it for you to make and maintain progress toward achieving this goal?

As if: When great leaders set their goals, they act as if they have already accomplished them, or as if they are happening right now. Henry Ford spoke about visualizing the combustion engine already working. How are you acting as if you already have achieved this goal?

Responsible: No one else is responsible for us achieving our goals. How are you going to hold yourself responsible for achieving this goal? What actions are you taking?

Toward: The language you use around goal setting is pivotal. Make sure to state your goal focusing on what you want to move closer toward, not on what you're moving away from or what you don't want.

Ecology: In NLP, we always check the ecology of an outcome or goal. This simply means being mindful of the consequences of making the changes you want and making sure that it's right for you and others involved. For example, one of my clients was working toward a promotion at work but didn't consider the impact the longer hours and travel demands would have on her family. In the end she felt it wasn't best for either her or her family to pursue the goal—it wasn't ecological. To check the ecology of your goal, ask yourself, *Is this right for me and the bigger picture I'm a part of? Will others be affected by this goal, and if so, how?*

Resources: We can easily forget how resourceful we actually are. What resources do you already have to achieve this goal? Maybe you've already got a foundation of knowledge, or you're determined, or you have a coach to support you.

Carve out some time to apply the SMARTER steps to a current goal. What difference does it make?

FURTHER THOUGHTS

- Check the simplicity of your goal by asking yourself, *How simple is it for me to tell others what I'm working toward?*
- To further check the ecology of your goal, explore how the immediate results of achieving this goal could be different from the long-term consequences.
- If you're not feeling very resourceful about achieving your goal, ask yourself, *What resources would I need? Where can I acquire those resources?*

3. Align Your Goals with Your Beliefs and Values

'I feel there's something missing here. You keep saying this is a goal that you *really* want to achieve, and yet week after week you're not taking the action steps you created toward it. Instead, you're coming up with every excuse under the sun. What's going on?'

Sidebar here: In my defense, this reads a lot harsher than it sounded in the actual conversation with my client! Although I'm a very caring and compassionate coach, I'm also good at noticing when people are standing in their own way, not being honest with themselves or not being congruent.

'You're right, Linda, and the bottom line is that I keep telling myself I want this goal, but actually I don't! I don't even care about having my own house. I don't even want to live at home, but it's what I feel I should do. It's what my friends have all done, it's what my sisters have done, and here I am—the black sheep. I don't care about saving. In fact, what I really want to do is blow all that money on travelling for a few months. Now that's what I really want.'

Bingo.

Sometimes the goals we set aren't even what *we* really want. They're the goals we feel we *should* set for ourselves, the goals our family would like to see us achieve, the goals that our friends are all working toward or have accomplished—but they're just not ours. When we set goals that are incongruent with who we are or what we want, we can easily end up self-sabotaging. We don't take action toward that goal and often end up at our own pity party thinking, *Why is this not working out for me?*

When you're setting goals for yourself you've got to make sure they are aligned with who you are and with what you want. Otherwise, nothing you do is going to make it work.

ACTION STEP

Choose a goal you've set for yourself and explore how that goal is aligned with your own values and beliefs by asking yourself, *What's important to me about achieving this goal? How is what I want congruent with my values?*

FURTHER THOUGHTS

When I first decided to quit smoking years ago, it didn't go very well and it took me some time to figure out why. I wasn't successful with this goal because I honestly didn't value my health at the time and prioritised being thin over everything. My "goal" of becoming a nonsmoker was never going to work until I changed how I felt about my health overall. The funny thing was that as soon as I decided to make my health a priority, quitting smoking became a lot easier. Something to think about if you're currently struggling to achieve a goal you've set for yourself.

Just Three Ways to Activate Your Own Happiness

H appiness could be:

    Enjoying a cold ice-cream on a hot day.

    Being warm and dry on a cold wet day.

Doing a job you absolutely love for a relatively low salary.

A married couple with no children and four rescue dogs.

Paying nearly $3,000 a month in rent to fulfil your dream of living in New York City. (Yes, this one is mine!)

Although happiness means different things to different people, the one thing we all have in common is that we want to be happy. A problem arises when we rely on other people or things to give us that feeling of being happy. Don't get me wrong, I believe there are times when being with other people or doing certain things can make us even happier, but it's our job to build the foundations to our happiness ourselves. That's one of the reasons I love the phrase "activate your own happiness". I feel it reminds us that it's our responsibility to take action steps toward building this foundation for ourselves too. That doesn't mean you can't be happy if you just be, because at that moment you might be actively focused on being present.

I spent most of my twenties trying to make myself happy and not always doing the best job of it. I tried and tested a number of things, but for me, the following three things have been—and continue to be—absolutely pivotal in helping me activate my own happiness.

1. Be Flawsome

No amount of self-improvement will make up for a lack of self-acceptance.

The first thing I encourage you to do in making progress toward your own happiness is to accept yourself. That means accepting who you are right now, accepting the choices you made, accepting that you're not perfect, accepting that you have flaws, and accepting that in spite of, or maybe because of, these flaws, you're still awesome in your own way. Stop fighting yourself and start embracing yourself instead.

If there's a part of you that you find hard to accept and you think it's easier to just ignore, newsflash: That's not going to help you in the long run. But accepting your flaws and taking action to create the change you want to see in yourself—that will help you. It's not about accepting the parts of ourselves we like and ignoring the rest; how's that going to work? It won't and you know it. It doesn't work to accept only 50 percent of ourselves or 80 percent of ourselves. Activating your own happiness is about you, all of you.

There were a number of times when I actually thought that by ditching certain parts of myself, or pretending they didn't exist, I could make myself happier. I wanted a fresh start. I didn't like certain attributes of the person I was at the time, but instead of facing up to these flaws and accepting them—because that sounded like way too much hard work—I thought it would be easier to just pretend they weren't there at all.

Sure, a fresh start is great, and you can make your own fresh start right here, right now, by choosing to accept your flaws, choosing to own your story, and seeing how it's empowered instead of weakened you.

Your first step to activating your own happiness is accepting you are flawsome.

(ACTION STEP)

Choose one of your "flaws" and consider how it has helped you at a certain point in your life.

FURTHER THOUGHTS

Every part of us is useful in a certain context. *Example:* I can be quite selfish and that has helped me set clear boundaries around my time, allowing me to complete assessments and write books. A really helpful way to begin accepting those parts of ourselves that we're not necessarily proud of is to look for the positive intent behind them.

- Although I'm not proud that I'm sometimes _____ it has helped me to _____.
- What do I appreciate about who I am?

- Instead of being critical of those parts of me, I can _____ instead. *Example:* I can continually beat myself up for making time for myself, or I can be grateful that this part of me even exists. I can choose to respect, appreciate, and even admire it.

2. Change Something That's Not Working

'I know this sounds kind of cheesy, Linda, but I just want to be happier, you know? I keep telling myself to just be happy!'

'And how's that working out for you?'

'Well, it's not, is it! I feel like I'm missing something. What's the secret? You must know, you're happy.'

I loved how Jane thought I had the secret!

One secret to activating our own happiness is to recognise what's not working and change it. After all, if you keep doing what you've always done, you'll keep getting what you've always got. Change something that's not working for you. To explain this piece better, I'm going to use the conversation I had with Jane in our session that day. You might find the questions I ask Jane useful for your own personal reflection too. They're deep and there are lots of them, but even just spending time on one a day can be incredibly helpful.

Me: You've said you want to be happier. What would that mean to you, Jane?

Jane: Gosh, I don't know, Linda, that's a big question. I feel like there would be less pressure on myself, for a start. It would mean I'd be content and not worrying as much. I worry a lot.

Me: Imagine we've a happiness scale of one to ten, with ten being super happy. How happy are you right now?

Jane: I'd say I'm a five on that scale.

Me: Great. And on that same scale of one to ten, where would you like to be?

Jane: Well we'd all love to be a ten, right? But I think even being at seven would make the world of difference to me.

Me: What stops you from moving further up that scale to where you want to be?

Jane: The pressure and the worry, Linda.

Me: And what are you going to do about that pressure and the worry?

Jane: Well they're clearly not working for me, are they? I put pressure on myself to get things done thinking then I'll be happy, but that doesn't work. And I worry about what might happen and that just saps any chance of happiness from me.

Jane and I continued our coaching conversation to see how she can begin to change the pressure she puts on herself and the worry habit she keeps herself in.

Bottom line, if you're not as happy in your own life right now as you want to be, what are you doing about it? Because you've always got the choice of leaving things as they are and hoping that they'll magically get better on their own, or you can act as the catalyst, take action, and begin to create the change you want.

What's a pattern of behaviour that holds you back from moving further up your own happiness scale? *Example:* Sometimes we might feel we have to be available to others and say yes to their requests, despite the fact that means we're saying no to ourselves.

FURTHER THOUGHTS

Sometimes we put up with things for the sake of a quiet life, but at what cost? There are so many things I've let slide over the years. Things bosses, ex-colleagues, old friends, close friends, have said to me because I wanted to avoid confrontation, but at a cost to my own peace of mind. Once I learned how to be more assertive, I changed that behaviour, realising it wasn't working for me. I recognised that voicing my own opinion was a way of demonstrating respect for myself.

- What are you putting up with?
- When are you saying yes when you'd prefer to be saying no?
- Where, or with whom, are you comfortable voicing your own opinion?

3. Ask Yourself, *What Am I available For?*

I absolutely love this question and find myself asking it frequently, especially whenever I get a request. I also love it in relation to activating my own happiness because it reminds me that I have a responsibility to myself to make myself happy, and how can I do that if I'm not clear about what it is I'm available for?

As an entrepreneur, I remember being told two very different pieces of advice by two very different people I greatly admired at the time.

'Never do anything for free, Linda. It reduces your credibility as a coach and does nothing for the coaching field in general. You must put a price on your work' was the first piece of advice.

'Never be afraid to do pro bono work. It can be a great way to get your name out there, and just because you're not getting money for it doesn't mean you're not getting anything in return. Just make sure it works for you too' was the second.

Years later, when I ask myself, *What work am I available for?*, my answer is simple: that which works for me and is aligned with my values, that's the work I'm available for.

What else am I available for? Time with Steve and my family, coffee/wine with wonderful friends, playing board games with my nieces and nephews, great conversations with great people, deep meaningful coaching sessions with my incredible clients, supporting people in their personal growth and professional development. I'm available for running, horse-riding, learning new things, supporting my own personal growth, and so much more.

I'm very clear on what I'm available for, and in the process of writing this book, I learned a lot about what I'm not available for either...

I was working away one day when I received an email from a radio show producer. She said one of her researchers had found me, watched the video of my story on my website, loved it, and thought I would be great for the show. Would I be available for a phone call with her within the next two weeks?

Sceptical, I checked out this radio show website and it was in fact, legit. So, as usual in Linda Land, I started getting really excited and my mind started racing ahead, culminating with me having my own radio show! I replied to my radio show lady and told her I was most definitely available for a phone call with her.

My radio show lady was wonderful to speak with. The show was part of an "Empowering Women" series and she sold it *very* well, to the point where thirty minutes into the conversation, I started wondering what the catch was. (There's my own impostor syndrome right there: *Why would such a high-profile show want me?*) And then came the catch: I had to pay for it. And what my radio show lady described as a "small fee", I would call something different! For a start, I'd call it nearly three return flights home. Sure, I was available to chat, I'll chat to anyone, but I won't pay for it. I get paid to talk and there will come a day when people will *pay me* a lot more than $1500 to be on their radio shows.

'Sorry, I'm not available for that at the moment. If anything changes I will definitely call you back. Thank you.'

ACTION STEP

Make a list of things that you're available for in your personal life. Think about people you're available for, activities you're available to participate in, places you're available to visit. What is worth you making time for?

FURTHER THOUGHTS

When we're not clear on what we're available for, we can end up saying yes to all kinds of things that we'd rather say no to.

* How easy do you find it to say no to others?
* Do you ever feel compelled to say yes to others to please them?
* Does this mean you're saying no to meaningful things that would serve you, in order to make time for requests from others you've felt you have to say yes to?

YOUR RELATIONSHIP WITH YOURSELF

Just Three Ways to Stop Comparing Yourself to Others

T hings must be so much easier for her. Why am I finding this so hard?

He seems to be much busier as a coach. Where is he getting all these clients?

Look at them, they're so lucky, I wish...

And just like that, I've fallen into the comparison thinking trap again, negatively comparing myself to others. In the past, I was stuck in this thinking trap. I compared every part of my life with that of others. I compared my looks—which frequently involved negative talk about my body, including everything from its size to getting my nose done—my running, where I lived and what I owned, my earnings, holidays, hotels... You name it and I negatively compared it to what others had.

I was so accustomed to being in this way of thinking that when I first set up my coaching business, I had three reminders stuck on the wall in my office and in my bathroom where I'd see them every day. After a few years they began to sink in! That's not to say I don't fall into the trap anymore because I still do, sometimes, but I'm much better at catching myself and getting myself right back out of it, and you will be too.

1. Compliment Yourself First

We can be really quick to compliment others and way too slow to compliment ourselves. A great first step in stopping that comparison thinking pattern is to catch yourself as soon as you recognise it's starting and compliment yourself instead. When I recognise I'm starting to compare my appearance negatively to others now, I compliment an aspect of myself. It might be something I'm wearing, or even the fact that I am proud that I didn't end up getting the nose job I was always harping on about. This can feel awkward at first, but stick with it because it's a lot better for our well-being than sitting in that compare and despair trap.

Another great way of complimenting yourself first is to write out a list of your skills, things you're proud of, and compliments people have given you or said about you on pieces of paper and pop them in a compliments jar. Then whenever you catch yourself making a negative comparison, take a piece of paper from your jar to remind yourself of how awesome you are. One of my clients also has a neighbouring comparison jar. Every time she catches herself negatively comparing, she makes a financial donation to the comparison jar! A client once told me about a kudos folder she created for herself where she keeps thank-you emails, words of recognition or praise, awards and accolades, etc, to remind herself of her good work.

Build up your own arsenal of successes—be it a compliment jar or a kudos folder—and have a dig around inside it whenever you start to fall into this way of thinking. Keep giving yourself a compliment each time you catch yourself in the comparison thinking trap. If you're stuck for ideas, refer back to your jar or folder for reminders of what other people have said about you.

FURTHER THOUGHTS

* How would your closest friends and loved ones describe you?
* What can others rely on you to do? *Example:* Maybe you're a wonderful listener or maybe you always lighten the mood with a funny story.
* What do you feel confident doing?

2. Remember It's a Highlight Reel, Not a Reality Reel

'I've noticed you don't do a lot of insta-stories except when you're travelling, Linda. I think people would love to see what you're up to each day in NYC and it would be great to develop your following; you're so SJP with your writing and everything.'

Ah, bless this wonderful woman's heart for her encouragement and kind words, but there are several reasons I don't do a lot of stories on my social media. First, just because I live in New York City does not mean my life is anything like *Sex and the City* at all. During the summer months, it's very much Sweat and the City and winter is very much Seven Sweaters and the City! New York herself is incredibly sexy all year round, of course. Second, I work—a lot; it's all part of being an entrepreneur, and if there's anyone out there really keen to see pics of me at my laptop, I think they need to have a long talk with themselves! Third, if I'm not at the laptop, I'm probably out running or curled up on the sofa roaring with laughter at my hilarious husband. Is that really story-worthy?

Jokes aside, social media continues to exacerbate the comparison trap. We scroll and compare, we scroll and complain, we scroll and forget that we're often scrolling through someone's highlight reel and not seeing the full picture. We get given a snapshot or a few seconds into someone's life and we suddenly feel as if we know their reality. It's all wonderful, sparkly, fun—and quite often filtered. Don't get me wrong, there are some fantastic people on social media who are all about keeping it real; I just think we need more of them.

ACTION STEP

One of my friends says he doesn't experience any negative comparisons when he uses social media because he has such a carefully curated list of people he follows. Maybe it's time to Marie Kondo your own accounts: If they don't spark joy, get rid of them!

FURTHER THOUGHTS

- What do you want people to think about you and your life? Why?
- What are the benefits of using social media? *Example:* Maybe it's ideas for your balcony garden, or cooking inspiration, or just a bit of downtime?
- How can you maximise on this instead of falling into the comparison trap?

3. Be Your Own Cheerleader

Along with thinking we're not doing enough, there's a myth floating around that it's not okay to cheer yourself on, to recognise your good work and be proud of it.

Newsflash! That's absolute BS! If anything, you've got to be your own cheerleader, and here's why.

As much as our family and friends care about our goals and want to see us doing well, they might not always know the ins and outs of the work we're doing behind the scenes, so we can't expect them to read our mind and know when we need cheering on. When we're our own cheerleaders we know exactly when we need that cheering on. This is also true of a personal goal we've not shared with others, or a goal that only we can see.

As your own cheerleader you can encourage yourself to take risks, stepping out of your comfort zone into your achievement zone. Remember that being your own cheerleader is a form of self-care: It's not about being arrogant, it's about being compassionate, encouraging, and motivating and appreciating all the effort you're putting into what you want to see in the world.

We're actually better able to support other people when we support ourselves first.

ACTION STEP

Be your own cheerleader today by recognising your successes from this day/week/month/year so far. If that feels like bragging and feels awkward, make it easier by being really specific. *Example:* I'm proud of this race I ran because I've been working so hard on my technique recently.

FURTHER THOUGHTS

Success takes many forms. It might be progress we've made, giving something another go, being compassionate with ourselves when things don't go according to plan.

- How are you rewarding yourself for all your efforts this week?
- What would you feel brave enough to do if you had someone cheering you on every step of the way?
- What's just one area where you feel you crave affirmation from other people?

Just Three Ways to Manage Your Inner Critic

Who am I even kidding? I'm just not good enough for this. *Who do you think you are to believe that you deserve this?*

People can see right through you, you know. They don't think you're an expert in anything!

Hello, inner critic, what do you want this time?

Our inner critic is that voice that just loves to tell us we're not good enough now and we never will be. It's that voice that feeds off our failures and loves to bring them up at any opportunity. It's that voice that belittles, criticises, judges, bullies, and just nags, nags, nags.

But the actual problem is the fact that we listen and even believe what that voice says; we often believe that we're not enough and we allow that belief to hold us back from facing our fears and doing what it is that we really want to do. *What will others think? People will think I'm stupid...* and we know how the record goes from there.

In an ideal world this wonderful inner critic wouldn't even

exist, now would it? But we don't live in that ideal world and if you're anything like me, you'll know full well that your inner critic isn't going away anytime soon. In fact, my critic often feels like she's on some lethal cocktail of energy pills and coffee, ready to party at the mere hint of me stepping outside my comfort zone! So, knowing that our inner critic is here to stay, what can we do about it?

1. Become an Objective Observer

It's impossible for us to change anything without awareness, so it's time to sit back, put your feet up, and just watch what goes on when your inner critic shows up. Imagine you're sitting in a movie theatre and your only job is to objectively observe the scenes you're about to see featuring your inner critic.

Just imagine that you've left your judgement at home and you've brought curiosity instead, as though you were watching a fascinating nature documentary about a rare beast.

From this place as objective observer, all you have to do now is notice how the critic shows up. Remember, you're just information gathering. There's no right or wrong, no good or bad, no judgement, and certainly no criticism.

What are some initial observations you notice about your inner critic? Write these down.

+ When does your inner critic usually show up?
+ How do you usually respond to the critic?
+ What questions pop into your head when it shows up?

2. Name It

'Her name is Joan-Ann, Linda. I have no idea where that name came from, but that's her name. She looks like a Joan-Ann too, you know?'

To be honest, I didn't know. I didn't know what a Joan-Ann looked like at all, but that's not important. What's important was that my client knew who this Joan-Ann was: She was her inner critic.

Naming our inner critic helps us manage it better because it gives us some power over it. By naming the critic, we can start to see what we're dealing with. We can shine a light on the critic and call it out instead of allowing it to hide away and taunt us. In naming the critic we also recognise that it's not our own voice of reason doing the criticising, which helps us separate ourselves from it objectively.

How did naming Joan-Ann help my client? She told me that she was able to recognise Joan-Ann more quickly and that alone empowered her. Naming her critic also reduced the seriousness of the criticisms because Joan-Ann now had a persona that my client found quite funny. 'She's that typical annoying aunt who likes to find fault with everything, you know? The one who asks why you're not married yet or the one who reminds you that as a woman your "clock" is ticking. God, she's annoying!' my client giggled.

(ACTION STEP)

Start to take control of your inner critic by naming it and giving it some kind of persona to help you gain control over it.

FURTHER THOUGHTS

- How do you feel about your own version of Joan-Ann?
- What's your first impulse when she turns up?
- How does Joan-Ann respond when you tell her to disappear? *Example:* Is it like trying NOT to think about pink elephants? How about when you greet her with friendliness but don't listen to what she has to say?

---

3. Change Aspects of the Voice

'Whose voice keeps criticising you here, because it certainly doesn't sound like you?' I asked a client one day as we worked to explore her inner critic.

'It's definitely my mother's voice, Linda. I can just hear her. She never seemed happy with what I did, always told me I made bad decisions. It's her—she's my bloody critic!'

Sometimes we might react to, or be triggered by, the voice alone of our inner critic, especially if it's someone we know personally, such as a parent or family member. We might find it's the words our inner critic uses that gets to us most, or it could be the tone that's used. Be curious and explore what it is about your critic's voice that really gets you, and then change aspects of that.

For example, with my client, we explored what difference it would make if her mother/inner critic sounded like her favourite cartoon character. As soon as I said that, my client burst out laughing because she suddenly heard her mother sounding like Marge Simpson, all worried and flustered. For her, this also changed the tone of the criticism because she said it sounded as if her mother was concerned and not critical—as Marge often was.

Notice what it is about your critic's voice that really triggers you, and change it to see what difference that makes.

FURTHER THOUGHTS

- If your inner critic likes to show up loudly, then imagine you can just turn the volume down on it as you would on a TV.
- If your inner critic likes to whisper in the background,

turn the volume up so you can have a proper conversation and find out what's going on with it.

- Compassion is a wonderful antidote for criticism. When that critical voice shows up, why not reply to it with self-compassion, care, and understanding?

Just Three Ways to Deal with Impostor Syndrome

"I have written 11 books, but each time I think, Uh oh, they're going to find out now. I've run a game on everybody, and they're going to find me out."

—Maya Angelou

Impostor syndrome. It's that fear of being found out, as though you're a fraud. That feeling that you don't measure up to others, or that sense that you don't deserve your success, because it really was pure luck. Hello, impostor syndrome, welcome back.

Despite the fact that the term was coined back in the '70s (and pertained particularly to women in high-powered positions) impostor syndrome is very much alive and well today and doesn't discriminate. Having to live with a nagging fear of being found out as not being as smart, talented, or experienced as people think is more common than we would think.

Personally, this is my Achilles heel. I feel I'm constantly battling it in so many areas of my life. As a history teacher, I felt like an impostor when my colleagues discussed sections of history that I had no idea about. And although I know it's completely irrational to think I can know everything about every chapter of history, it only takes one simple *Oh, you know nothing about that!* thought to set the impostor syndrome wheel of negative thoughts in motion.

I felt like an impostor the first time I got my first paying coaching client. *Who are you to charge people for this?!* I felt like a fraud when I started mentoring other coaches during their coach training. *They'll find out, you know!* I even felt like a fraud when I started talking openly about my own challenges around mental health. *You've still got so much of your own sh*t going on and you're presenting that you've got it sorted? Fraud!*

And impostor syndrome goes into complete overdrive when we prepare to put ourselves out there for the whole world to see and to judge. My impostor syndrome had an absolute field day when I set about writing my first coaching book. *Who are you to be writing this book? You're from a small town in the west of Ireland; you're not this glamourous best-selling author in New York's Upper East Side, you know. Back in your box!*

Fraud, fraud, fraud.

That's what impostor syndrome is, but how can we deal with it?

1. Know What You Bring to the Table (and What You Don't)

Imagine offering to host a five-course dinner party for about twenty people where you have to cook everything yourself... but you regularly burn toast.

Good idea or bad idea?

Cooking for large groups of people is most definitely not my forte; even just thinking about it sets the hamster wheel of anxious thoughts going in my head.

But what would happen in the same situation if your guests offered to bring something that would make the evening run more smoothly? If you know that Tom loves making desserts and is fantastic at it, why not ask him if he could make one for the evening instead of bursting into a panic over pavlova? And if Ailsa, as a sommelier, has offered to pick up some red wine that will pair perfectly with your main course, why not let her, instead of pretending you know your malbec from your merlot? And I will gladly volunteer my services as quiz master extraordinaire!

I was once asked, 'In terms of this team project, what can we rely on you to do, Linda?' And although I wanted to say I could handle it all on my own because I really wanted to impress the person I was sitting across from, I knew that a) that wasn't the case in terms of the time frame, and b) I knew that someone else on the team could definitely manage the marketing aspect much better than I could. So knowing what I could positively and confidently bring to the table, I identified an aspect of the project where I could use my expertise and then recommended another team member as the marketing expert. Not only was my project leader impressed with my role as a team player, but my colleague was also grateful I had highlighted their marketing prowess.

Make a list of all the things you're brilliant at or just love doing and identify where you currently use those in your personal and professional life.

FURTHER THOUGHTS

Be mindful that impostor syndrome will often bring limiting beliefs such as, *I need to be able to do it all*, or, *As an expert in this area, I should know everything about it*, to the surface. These beliefs can easily spark off a train of unhelpful thoughts if we don't catch them in time: *What will people think of me if I don't know the answer? What will my boss think if I say I can't do this part of the project?* But knowing what you bring to the table—and what you don't—helps quieten thoughts of self-doubt, and voicing it helps create a culture of safety and vulnerability in your workplace.

2. Own Your Successes

'I'm not good in interviews, Linda, you know? It just feels like bragging when I'm asked about my current success.'

'Where have I been successful recently? Gosh, I don't know. I wouldn't describe anything I've done recently as successful because I've been unemployed for so long.'

'I find it really hard to accept the praise from my boss, because it was a team effort.'

From labelling it as "bragging", believing it's context specific, and being unwilling to see individual contribution to team success, there are three big challenges to owning our successes that I frequently hear.

First, owning our success will never feel right if we label it as bragging. But recognising the hard work and effort put into something isn't bragging. Owning our success is made all the more challenging if we've grown up with the belief that it's wrong to talk about your successes. But there's a huge difference between the two. Compare the statement of, 'Well, if not for me the project would have been a complete failure; nobody else had a clue what they were doing' with, 'I worked really hard on that project. It was incredibly challenging at times and that's what makes it stand out as one of my successes'. The first statement is bragging and even belittles other people, which is never going to go down well, whereas the second statement emphasises effort and identifies challenges; it's authentic and you can even hear it being said in a very different tone.

Second, owning our success is also harder if we believe it's context specific. For example, if Pete only associates success with paid employment and he's been unemployed for some time, it's no wonder he's blind to his other successes, because in his world, success comes with work. Success can happen in any context; it just may not always be so obvious because of how we define it, but that doesn't mean it doesn't exist. In fact, because success is so subjective, it's even more important that you recognise, embrace, and own yours.

Third, when it comes to a group or team effort, we may find it harder to own our successful contribution if we feel that doing so downplays or diminishes the role of others. Who says that in recognising my contribution, I'm making less of my colleagues' great work? No one! If you're susceptible to this limiting belief around success, you can work around it by highlighting the successful facts or details instead of making generic comments. For example, 'I feel everyone really pulled together on this one. Sarah's planning and focus was strategic, Joe's content was hard-hitting, and I was pleased with my design ideas. It's a great feeling.'

Remember that there are all sorts of ways of thinking about success. What does it mean for you? Some people believe that success is measured in wealth accumulated or return on investments made. Other people measure success in terms of physical challenges overcome and progress made toward a goal, whereas others see success in terms of creating and maintaining strong relationships.

Success might be about learning a lesson and finally applying it! It could be about changes you've made in order to grow personally and professionally; challenges you've overcome; confidence you've gained; skills you've acquired; knowledge gained; relationships built, strengthened, and fostered... The list is endless.

(ACTION STEP)

Catch yourself next time you fall into one of the three traps listed previously that are barriers to owning your success.

- Talking about successes sometimes feels like bragging. What does it feel like to you?
- What are some of your successes that you're quick to ignore or brush over?
- When do you find it harder to accept compliments or praise?

3. Aim for Progress, Not Perfection

Impostor syndrome loves nothing more than a perfectionist because that's where it can really thrive. It just loves to show up and remind us how we're falling short of perfection over and over again. It feeds off the negative comparisons, the self-doubt, and the unrealistic expectations that striving for perfection creates. This is why you'll serve yourself much better by aiming to make progress instead of striving for perfection.

I'm reminded of a conversation I had with my client, Dan, about this issue, which went like this:

Dan: I've got to get this job, Linda, so my interview tomorrow has got to go perfectly.

Me: What does that mean?

Dan: You know, I have to get everything right. It's got to be perfect. At this stage, I *should* be able to nail these interviews, I've done enough of them.

Alarm bells had already gone off in my head with the first *perfectly* and now with *should* added to the mix, oh my word!

Me: When you focus on trying to get things perfect, how do you feel?

Dan: I'm a nervous wreck, look at me! I haven't slept properly all week. I keep thinking of things I don't know, interview questions I haven't practiced... Even in my current role I feel like I'm not as good as the other team members. They've all been to outstanding universities and I'm sure they wonder how I got a job there.

Me: What's the meaning you place on getting things perfect?

Dan: It means I'm good enough. It means I could perhaps stop comparing myself to the other team members. Trying to get things perfect so no one will have anything to criticise— they won't find out what I don't know. But even just saying that out loud sounds ridiculous. Why am I so afraid of being found out? It's like I'm ashamed that I didn't have the private school and fancy university upbringing that many of the other candidates did, and then I'm ashamed that I feel that way.

Me: You know what I love? I love that you're actually where those other candidates are, even though you didn't have that upbringing. Look how far you've come, look at how hard you've worked and the progress you've made to get here!

Dan: That's hilarious. When you put it like that, that I'm at the same place as they are, going for the same job, that says a lot, doesn't it?

Our conversation carried on where my client knew it was

going to serve him best not to focus on getting things perfect but to focus on how far he had come. Dan realised he could choose to go into that interview with a chip on his shoulder about not having had such a privileged education, or he could focus on his professional progress.

You'll serve yourself much better when you aim for progress instead of perfection when you focus on the growth, personal and professional, that you've made rather than what you've not done or not achieved.

Make it progress over perfection. Every time.

ACTION STEP

Choose an aspect of your life and take a minute to reflect on all the progress you've made in that area over the last twelve months.

FURTHER THOUGHTS

- What were you quick to notice about the last twelve months in that area of your life?
- What were you slower to notice? Sometimes we can be quick to criticise, quick to see what we don't have or what we didn't achieve instead of what we did.
- What progress would someone else have seen that maybe you've missed?

Just Three Ways to Improve
Your Self-Confidence

I struggled with self-confidence for years and truth be told, I still struggle with it today. It's ironic because many people I know would describe me as being confident. When I've asked them what gives them that impression, they often tell me it's because they've seen me speak in public and for many people that's an indicator of having confidence—across the board. They're usually flabbergasted when I've then told them how I might appear confident on a stage, but the reality is that my heart is pounding and I'm sweating profusely underneath that calm-looking exterior. Isn't it interesting what we assume to be true about others?

I've made the same assumption about others too. I once worked with a client whom I considered to be quite naturally confident, to the point that when she requested to work with me to develop her confidence for an upcoming speaking event, I couldn't understand why. *Why does she need me?* I wondered. But then I realised that my client's event was terrifying her. For weeks beforehand she couldn't sleep. She had nightmares about it, and her head was filled with those pesky what-if thoughts of anything and everything that could go wrong. She was so anxious she was close to cancelling her opportunity to speak. What I found most intriguing was that when I asked her what she did have the confidence to do, she said she never had any problem hosting or cooking for huge numbers of people. 'I just know what to do when I'm in the kitchen.'

What I find when I work with my clients on this particular issue is that low self-confidence doesn't usually affect all areas of our lives, only some of them. Some of us might be terrified of speaking in public but think nothing of cooking a four-course meal for twenty people. And if you're confident in some things, then you can be confident in others, right? The confidence is there; it's about bringing it out when we need it.

1. Go First

If you think of your confidence like a muscle that you'd like to define and strengthen, then you know you've got to exercise it regularly and consistently.

This doesn't mean that you have to jump out of your comfort zone to go sky-diving one week and climb Kilimanjaro the next, but it does mean consciously looking for ways to keep flexing that confidence muscle. One way we can do this is by going first. If you've ever been in a situation, such as standing in an elevator or a queue, and you'd really like to strike up a conversation with another person there but you've been too nervous to go first, then you'll know exactly what I mean. We sometimes stand or sit there, hoping the other person will go first so we don't have to, but going first is a great way to step—as opposed to jump—outside your comfort zone. Sure, there's always a chance it won't go well and you might get just a smile in return, but if you don't go first you'll never know.

I used to hate going to networking meetings. I used to hate talking to absolute strangers about what I do and why I do it. I also knew that if I didn't go and speak to new people, how were they going to find out about me and what I do? I decided that if I was going to get comfortable talking to strangers, then I better get talking to strangers, so that's what I did. I set myself the task of speaking to two strangers every day. I spoke to strangers in a queue, in an elevator, or anywhere I had the opportunity to do so, and if the opportunity wasn't there immediately, I created it myself by going first.

I'd go first by simply smiling or saying hello. I often broke the ice by complimenting the other person, and we all love a compliment, don't we? I've experienced many kinds of reaction to doing this and they've all been really positive so far. I remember one day, after a bit of a rubbish meeting, meeting a gentleman in the elevator who looked like he'd also just had a bad meeting, so I said hello to him and he was delighted I did. 'You have no idea how many times I see the same people in this elevator every single day and rarely does anyone smile at each other, let alone say hello. You've made my day, thank you.' As scary as it can be, sometimes we need to be the one to go first.

ACTION STEP

Make the commitment to yourself this week to step outside your comfort zone and go first with something you've been putting off.

FURTHER THOUGHTS

- As you think of an upcoming situation where you'd like to have more confidence, what's something you can do in the next few days to prepare for it?
- What are some of your strengths and how can you use those to give you a confidence boost? One of my strengths is humour and just thinking about my ability to make others smile or have a giggle gives me a confidence boost.
- What is it that stops you from going first and how can you face that? Many people don't go first out of fear of what the other person will think of them. Clients ask me all the time, 'What if I say something stupid? What will they think of me?' I always reply with, 'So what if you say something stupid? Embrace it. You might be the only one who thinks it's stupid and the other person might find it hilarious.'

2. Get Competent

We all know at least one person who has more confidence than competence! That person who assertively tells the ski instructor that they don't need to do the beginner's training because they "know what to do". And of course, we all know this translates to: They've never actually been on a mountain covered in snow before, but they've seen in it the movies, how hard can it be?!

Competence, or the know-how to do something, gives us confidence, but confidence doesn't always give us competence. If we want to build up our confidence in a particular area, getting more knowledgeable about the topic will help us immensely.

Get competent about your topic. Get competent about the content for your upcoming presentation. Get competent for that pending interview, because that gives you confidence. Speak to people who are already in the know, ask better questions, and carry out research to fill some gaps in your knowledge, so you can speak about your topic with confidence.

One of the things that used to hold me back from speaking to people at networking events was a fear of being asked a question about coaching or NLP that I wouldn't know the answer to. What would I do? I felt that I couldn't admit I didn't know the answer because then people wouldn't hire me; they'd think I was a fraud or stupid. However, while I continue to become the best coach I possibly can be and that has made me more competent, it's also given me the confidence to say 'I don't know' to something. Confidence isn't about knowing everything, because that's unrealistic. Confidence is about being comfortable in your own skin, being comfortable with what you know, and being comfortable to say what you don't know yet either.

ACTION STEP

What one thing would you like to be more competent at? Choose one way of developing that competence today.

FURTHER THOUGHTS

- What do you feel most competent doing?
- Where do you feel confident to say that you don't know something?
- And where, if anywhere, do you not feel comfortable admitting what you don't know?

3. Fake It Until You Make It

I'm a good horse rider. I'm not Olympic standard, but I've always loved watching professional riders. In fact, I've always loved watching professional athletes compete in their disciplines. From swimmers to skiers and boxers to runners, for me, they all have one thing in common and that's how they approach their starting line. I'm not talking about their years of training and sacrifice, but how they physically approach their mark. You don't see these athletes sluggishly make their way to the blocks or the ring. Instead, you see them move with purpose; you see them walk like they're already victorious, their bodies radiating confidence. No matter how they're feeling inside, they know they've got to rock up looking like they own it.

You've probably heard of power poses as a way to instill confidence when you need it. Amy Cuddy, a social psychologist at Harvard Business School, found that taking up a short power pose, an open and expansive stance (think Wonder Woman, Superman, etc.), can actually change body chemistry and make people feel more confident. Yes, I'm aware that the science of these power poses is an ongoing study, but the evidence is there to show that in many cases, changing your physiology does change how you feel.

You don't see people in powerful positions walk to their own starting line with slouched shoulders and heads hanging low, hell no! They know that they're judged on their appearance from the first glance, before they've even opened their mouth, and so looking the part is crucial.

And this is true for any of we mere mortals too: If you want to project confidence and power in any aspect of your life, then first you've got to feel it, and if you don't feel it naturally, you can fake it until you do.

An experience that always helps me trigger confidence is remembering simple instructions I was once given by my riding instructor: 'Sit tall and proud on your horse, Linda, shoulders back and head up. Imagine there's a tiny thread attached to the crown of your head and someone is gently pulling it up, encouraging you to sit taller.' And that's exactly what I do when I want to feel confident—I change my physiology. I sit, or stand, tall and proud with my head up and my shoulders back. I don't need to be on the horse to feel that confidence— by simply changing my posture and holding those confident thoughts, my chemistry naturally changes.

ACTION STEP

Try this three-minute exercise. Think of a time when you felt most confident. As you think of that time, remember what you were doing and what was happening around you. Really immerse yourself in that memory, seeing what you saw at the time, hearing what you heard—get as many details of the memory as you possibly can and allow that confidence to be reignited in you. As you feel that confidence coming back to you, notice how it's different to be fully present in that confident state. Easy, right? And all you're doing is pretending.

FURTHER THOUGHTS

- Power poses are based on modelling confident behaviour. What does confidence look like to you?
- Who do you consider to be confident and why?
- How would life be different for you if you had more self-confidence?

3

DEALING WITH
OTHERS

Just Three Ways to Respond Rather than React

'Hi, Linda, just a gentle reminder that your reports are due at three p.m. today...'

Just a "gentle reminder"? Have you any idea of the day I'm having and the week I've had so far? Have I ever missed a deadline yet? Nope! So, let me give you a gentle reminder right now!

Cue the absolute indignation building inside me as my fingers type furiously on the keyboard in preparation to tell this person what I really think of their "gentle reminder" and their stupid report deadlines too. And that, my friends, is the perfect example of me reacting rather than responding. If you've read the first couple of chapters in this book already, you'll know that choosing to respond rather than react is something I continually work on, because I still take things really personally.

Reacting is immediate and fuelled by emotion—just like me in the preceding example. In comparison, responding is thoughtful, logical, and objective. Choosing to respond rather than react to situations empowers us because it gives us choice, and choice is always better than no choice. Yes, I know that in certain situations this is definitely easier said than done, so, if you're a little bit fiery like me and you can easily take things personally, this section is especially for you.

And for what it's worth, I never did send that email.

1. Move Away from the Situation

A simple yet powerful step to help you respond instead of react immediately is to hit the pause button. Move away from that message, from the email, from your laptop, from the person. You might not have access to a beautiful beach or forest to visit and regain your zen, so it's fine if all you can do is move away from your desk or computer for a few seconds. It's what you do in that time that counts.

Give yourself this time to look at what you can control about the situation. If it's just your breath, that's good enough. Slow down your breath, inhaling control deeply and slowly exhaling that frustration, anger, uncomfortable emotion. By moving away, you're already in a different place where you can manage yourself better.

Know that at any point in time, you can always move away mentally too. Close your eyes and see yourself in a much more empowered, controlled state. Deeply inhale confidence, calm, patience, or whatever resource you need, then slowly exhale whatever resource is not helpful in that situation.

Moving away physically or mentally allows us to break that negatively charged state before we react in a way that will create more problems. It's about gaining control over the frustration so it doesn't control you. It's about being in the position to choose a better response rather than a knee-jerk reaction.

Take some time to recognise your own triggers: those people or situations that make you want to react instinctively instead of respond thoughtfully. For me and my clients, these often tend to include things like emails from someone leading a project or from a boss, personal criticisms instead of constructive criticism about the work done, etc.

FURTHER THOUGHTS

- What choices do you have in terms of how you respond to this situation or person?
- How would you like to be able to respond in these trigger situations?
- What's just one thing you could do differently to help you achieve that better outcome?

2. Gain a Different Perspective

How could they not see where I'm coming from?
This is absurd! I can't believe they don't see this!
Am I the only one who sees what an absolute disaster this is?

We don't see things as they are, we see things as *we* are. When we get caught up in a reactive situation we're often blinded by our own values and beliefs, unable to see how others don't agree with them.

My client Sandra told me about a frustrating situation she often found herself in. Whenever Sandra, her husband, and their two children travel home to see her parents in the UK, Sandra's dad usually has their few days there all planned out—without consulting Sandra. 'It's like he still sees me as this child who can't organise things herself, Linda. It's so frustrating! How does he think I cope as a working mum?' It was getting to the stage where Sandra was ready to blow up and tell her father exactly what she thought of his "plans". I took Sandra through the following exercise to help her gain a better perspective.

The Gaining a New Perspective exercise is great for helping us see things from a different point of view. It's one I use frequently on my own and with clients. This exercise is adapted and used with permission from MindBridge® Trainings.

Step 1: Label three separate markers (I use basic index cards, but use whatever you want) with Self, Other, and Observer. Set these three markers on the ground in a triangle, a comfortable distance apart for the space you have.

Step 2: Position one, Self, is all about your own experience of the situation. When you step onto this marker, think about the situation and your reaction to it. Be aware of how you're standing, your thought process, and any feelings that emerge. In my experience, people rarely have to spend a long time in this first position before feeling those uncomfortable emotions come back to them, which is what immediately happened to Sandra.

Step 3: Step off the Self marker and into a neutral space outside the triangle. The purpose of this is to "break the state" or disconnect from those uncomfortable emotions before moving to the second position. Here, I asked Sandra to do something unemotional, such as saying her phone number backward, because it's helpful for breaking the state and redirecting your focus.

Step 4: Position two, Other, represents the other person in the situation. Here, it's Sandra's dad. When you're ready, step onto that marker. Your objective here is to step into this person's shoes as best as you can, to see the situation through their own experience. It's important to give yourself time and notice what you observe about the situation from this position. (This is where having someone else help you with the exercise can prove particularly useful.) From this position, I asked Sandra, 'What do you notice about your dad and what he wants from this position?' Sandra immediately burst into tears, saying that she realised that all her dad wanted was to spend time with her and her family. He wasn't being malicious, it was his love for her as a dad and for her kids as a grandfather. 'They see him once or twice a year and he loves them so much,' she told me.

What's important to this person in this situation? Some people find it helpful to take on the posture or body language of the other person too.

- As the other person, how do you feel about the situation?
- What do you notice about person one from this position?
- What do they want? What do you want?

Step 5: Repeat step 3 to clear your mind again.

Step 6: Position three, Observer, represents a neutral person, someone completely unattached to the situation. Think of someone you know who would give you an honest, unbiased observation of the current situation—Sandra chose a close friend of hers—and when you're ready, step onto that marker as that person. From this third position as the observer, how do you see the person in position one?
- How do you see the person in position two?
- From this neutral position, what do you notice about both people?
- What do you notice about the situation that the other two people don't see or maybe can't see from their positions?

Step 7: When you're ready, step out of the Observer position, clearing your mind in the same way as before.

This is a really powerful exercise that helps us take on different positions, enabling us to see things from different perspectives. When we're truly open to this, we also gain greater choice in how we respond to a situation rather than react immediately to it.

(ACTION STEP)

Carry out the Gaining a New Perspective exercise to help you respond better to a current event or situation you're still finding challenging. This is also a great exercise to help you manage how you feel about an event from your past.

FURTHER THOUGHTS

- In the exercise, what was most challenging for you about being in position two, Other?
- Did you find being the Observer or the Other hardest? Why?
- What can these findings tell you about your interactions with others? *Example:* If we find it challenging to be in the role of Other, it can be an indication that a little more empathy from our side could be helpful.

3. Ask Yourself,
What could be true here?

Imagine that a good friend turns to you one day and comments that you've been quite negative and cynical recently.

How do you react?

Do you give a knee-jerk, defensive reaction, saying it's them and not you? After all, they're the ones who live in LaLa Land thinking that everything is great all the time. Or do you press pause and step away from the situation? (See page 116.) In that pause, could you consider what could be true about the comment your friend made?

This happened to me recently and my knee-jerk reaction was to be defensive. Me, negative? And cynical? Is she for real? I think she's the one who is Little Miss Negativity here! That nuclear-reactor-me, ready to defend myself to the hilt, was never willing to consider that my friend's statement might have had the slightest hint of truth to it. And why? Because even considering it meant that perhaps I had become cynical recently, and that would mean I wasn't the ray of sunshine and positivity I wanted to see myself as. I left the conversation pretty abruptly but couldn't help thinking, *Shell is a really good friend. Could there be some truth to what she said?*

When I gathered the courage to explore what could be true about what my friend said in a compassionate way, I was surprised to see the truth that was there. I was also ashamed of the way I'd behaved, and that's hard to say. My friend was right; I had become quite negative and cynical.

The truth about ourselves can be hard to see and accept at times, there's no denying that, but if we're not open to it, how can we learn more about ourselves, what triggers us and how to respond better?

A few days later, I went to speak to Shell. I thanked her for being so honest and said I was unaware of how I'd been behaving and how that had been experienced by others. We ended up having a really great conversation and I respect her so much for helping me hold that mirror up.

(ACTION STEP)

Take an uncomfortable comment or piece of feedback you've received recently and ask yourself what could be true about it?

FURTHER THOUGHTS

- What can you learn about yourself from this feedback?
- How can you explore this truth with kindness and compassion?
- What could be the positive intent behind sharing the feedback?

Just Three Ways to Deal with a Difficult Boss

I have always found it challenging to work for people I don't respect. It was just so hard for me. I couldn't understand when people didn't do their job properly, when they turned a blind eye to an obvious problem, pretended not to know what was going on, or pointed the finger of blame at someone else instead of taking responsibility for their own actions. I can feel my frustration building just typing these words! And I could never understand how other people didn't let it bother them. That in itself used to bother me. Why weren't other people calling my boss out on their sh*t? Why do some people just say nothing? No wonder one boss commented that I didn't handle frustration very well—because I didn't.

Unless you plan on quitting your day job and becoming your own boss, it's in your best interest to develop a better relationship with the person you report to. And if just uttering those words makes you roll your eyes, then you've come to the right place! Use this section to help you develop some self-management tools to help you deal with an "interesting" boss or colleague.

1. Re-label Them

I once worked for this guy who—how shall I put this nicely?—didn't have the greatest leadership skills. Many of us often sat in meetings, internally eye-rolling, cringing, and just wanting to shout, 'Please just shut up, PLEASE!' It was like he forgot he was speaking to a group of adults when he spoke to the team in his patronizing, arrogant manner and then wondered why the team didn't jump to his every command. But let's not judge. The majority of the staff thought he was absolutely bonkers and rarely listened to a word he said. They were often nice to his face but then spent the next few hours bitching and moaning about comments or demands he had made. When I had a run-in with him one day that left me seething with rage, I knew I had to do something different to turn this around or I wasn't going to last very long in my workplace—and I loved my job.

I walked into the staff room one day where my colleagues were standing around literally agog at this guy's latest faux pas, saying, 'He said what?' 'I cannot believe it!' 'What's going to come out of his mouth next?!' I joined in the conversation. My question was, 'Why are we all surprised at this stage by this guy? It's the same thing over and over again. His behavior is so predictable. His words might not be, but his behavior is textbook.'

'You don't seem bothered by this, Linda, not even after the way he treated you the other day. How do you do it? I'd be still fuming,' one of my colleagues said to me. Then I let her in on a little secret.

'When you think of this guy, what label pops into your head straight away?' I asked her.

'Honestly, I think he's spineless,' she said.

'Okay. That's interesting, because I call him The Entertainer, and the label alone reduces so much of the frustration I used to feel.'

'What? How?' My colleague was intrigued.

'Think about it logically. We gasp and cringe at the stuff that comes out of his mouth, and we've no idea what he's going to say next. It's almost like a game show—he's an entertainer!'

By changing the label you place on people, you can begin to change how you feel about them. I'm not saying you have to like them; this is about doing something to serve you better that makes your day more manageable. Moreover, it might even keep you from getting caught up in the staffroom chat about them too, which would probably lead to you being more productive overall—winner winner!

Change the label you place on people and you change your perspective.

ACTION STEP

Choose a person in your life that you would like to feel less frustrated by and re-label how you see that person so you can manage yourself better around them.

FURTHER THOUGHTS

Changing the label I placed on my boss was the step I took, and that in itself worked well in terms of reducing my frustration. Being a highly visual person, I then started to imagine my boss wearing a t-shirt that said "Entertainer" on it. From there, I went a step further and imagined they were wearing some kind of an entertainer's outfit too—in this case, it was a clown suit, which worked brilliantly and ties in beautifully with the next technique.

2. The Circus Music Technique

I love to use this trick, and it's something I've also used along with the re-labelling technique I just described. If you've already read the section on dealing with your past (page 43), you'll be familiar with the whole idea of submodalities in NLP. If you've jumped straight in here, let me give you a quick synopsis of what these submodalities are: When we picture things that have happened in the past or things that could potentially happen in the future, those images will have a number of components that in NLP we call submodalities. Visually, these submodalities describe how we see experiences; is the image still like a photo or moving like a movie scene? Is the image clear or blurry? There might be auditory submodalities associated with the image, such as someone speaking softly or loudly, or background noise. And there could be a kinesthetic element to the image too, such as a sensation we feel when we think about the event. Think about it logically; if someone asked you to relive a particularly scary event, you might shiver and begin to feel the hairs on the back of your neck stand up, or when you think about a really happy memory, you might immediately start smiling as you picture yourself there again, reliving the event.

Imagine I've had a run-in with my boss and it's replaying over and over again in my head, as we often do with negative experiences. Imagine that when I think about the event, it runs like a short movie clip but on a big screen so it's all really clear and vivid. I can hear his patronizing words and tone and I can see the smug look on his face, which makes me want to punch him. Scenes like this can be frustrating even just to think about. Logically, I know that if I allow that scene to replay over and over again in my head, it's not going to be good for me; I'll probably end up feeling worse and maybe saying or doing something I'll regret, so here's what I can do instead.

We already know how re-labelling a person can immediately change how we feel about them—like seeing my old boss as an entertainer. To further reduce those negative thoughts and the frustration I felt about my boss, I also imagined him dressed in a circus clown costume.

Now, as I replay that scene in my head, I'll press play on some circus music: some really loud, daft circus music. I'll focus on the massive clown suit he's wearing, the bright green wig, the painted-on clown face that conceals that smug look, and I'll hear the entertaining circus music. I'll focus on the ridiculousness of the whole scene and throw some other elements into the mix to really emphasise the entertainment value, to the point where I'm no longer bothered about what he actually said to me at the time. You can do this as often as you need to reduce the uncomfortable emotions you once had attached to the scene/person.

How do you know if it works? As with any of this material, test it. If you feel better about the situation, it works! If you still feel frustrated, that's a sign to do something different.

Play around with the sounds or soundtrack from your old memories that may still cause you some discomfort, adding or subtracting whatever makes the scene more manageable for you.

FURTHER THOUGHTS

- Music is powerful and can trigger strong emotions. What kind of music makes you want to get up and move?
- What music makes you feel a little mischievous?
- What song makes you feel invincible?

3. Look at the Positive Intention of Their Behaviour

Sure, you can see what your boss is doing wrong, your colleagues can see what their boss is doing wrong, even the DHL delivery person can see what your boss is doing wrong—everyone can see it, except your boss. And even if they do have the ability to see the negative effects their behaviour has on the staff, they might not think there's anything wrong with it: "It's not me, it's you".

You can spend your time wishing your boss did things differently, but you can't force them to change. What you can do is manage yourself better and focus on controlling the control-lable. One way to manage yourself better in a situation like this is to look for the positive intention in your boss's behaviour.

Something that often frustrates my clients when I dis-cuss this idea of positive intention is the fact that the boss's behaviour clearly doesn't have a positive impact and serves no purpose. But that's the thing about understanding the positive intent behind a particular behaviour: It's not about the impact the behaviour has on other people, it's about what the person carrying out the behaviour stands to get, gain, or achieve as a result. Your boss might behave in a particular way to exert power over others, to show themselves in a better light, to show superiority, etc. This doesn't mean others are positively impacted by the behaviour at all, but the do-er gains something from their actions. It's the same for the boss who passes off someone else's work as their own to show themselves as being competent, or who uses threats as a way of motivating their staff. Not positive behaviours at all, but there's a positive intent behind them. I'm not condoning your boss's behavior; I'm saying that people choose to behave the way they do because they see something valuable to be gained from it.

When we learn to take a step back and ask ourselves what someone could be hoping to get or gain from their behaviour, we get a better idea of what could be going on for them. And I don't know about you, but when I try this idea of positive inten-tion on for size, I usually end up feeling sorry for the person in question. The boss who feels the need to belittle others, the person who patronises others, the person who spends their time driving their souped-up car around the estate... it's sad really. Perhaps your boss is seeking power or control, perhaps they feel they have to establish themselves, perhaps this is what they believe a boss has to do. Perhaps they don't actually know any better. After all, remember that we don't know what we don't know and we won't know until someone teaches us.

Think of someone's behaviour, or even just a behaviour in general, that you find really annoying or frustrating. Imagine a scenario where you can see the behaviour taking place and notice what's coming up for you.

Now step back from that scenario in your mind (some people find it helpful to remove themselves from it completely) and imagine that you're now looking at the scene through the lens of every behaviour having a positive intent. Notice what's different about the scenario for you.

FURTHER THOUGHTS

If you work with young people or you have children, this is a great exercise to do with them, using a pair of imaginary positive intention frames to view the situation through. *Example:* 'Pop on these positive intention frames for me for a minute and think about a positive reason why that person did what they did. What could they be trying to get for themselves?'

Just Three Things to Consider When Dealing with Feedback

F eedback is one of the most crucial requirements for personal growth or professional development, so why do so many of us cower from it? If we know it can help us: teach us, make us feel good, and even support our flourishing in life, what stops us seeking it more often than we do? Fear of judgement from others, our own limiting beliefs about feedback, or seeing it as a personal attack prevent us being open to receiving feedback and therefore closed to learning and growth. Whereas not wanting to hurt others, fear of repercussions, or simply not having the communication skills prevent us being able to deliver feedback effectively.

Until I learned to see feedback as a growth mechanism, I absolutely hated getting any. The very mention of the word *feedback* and I was on the defensive, ready to ride off into the sunset, oblivious to whatever was about to be said to me! If it wasn't all positive, I simply didn't want to hear it. I'm laughing to myself as I write this because it sounds so absurd when I think of all the personal growth and development I've gone through over the years. The following three things on feedback have been pivotal in helping me make that change, and I know when you're open to considering them, you'll find them helpful in the feedback process too.

1. Be Aware of Your Beliefs about Feedback

It's just an opportunity for someone to judge you.

He doesn't like me, so he's obviously not going to give me any positive feedback.

Whenever anyone asks if they can give you feedback you know it's not going to be good.

Those were three of my own beliefs about feedback before I discovered NLP. You don't need to be a rocket scientist to see how limiting those beliefs are, right? If I believe I'm going to be judged, that the other person won't be professional, or that it's going to be a completely negative conversation, then of course I'm not going to be open to feedback.

We've gathered and built a set of beliefs about all aspects of life from when we were very young, but as we grow up, we rarely make the time to check in and evaluate how useful those beliefs still are to us.

Three beliefs I have about feedback now are these:

- It's essential for my own learning and growth.
- There's always something to be learned from feedback.
- Feedback is necessary for my own self-awareness.

This set of updated beliefs is clearly more empowering. When I keep these at the forefront of my mind during any feedback experience, not only am I honouring my own desire to grow, but I'm also in a much better position to manage myself and my emotions if the conversation gets uncomfortable.

When it comes to feedback, whether you're required to deliver it or you're on the receiving end, make sure that you're aware of the beliefs you hold around it and ensure those beliefs serve both you and the other person involved.

Make a list of your own beliefs around feedback, exploring how helpful they are to you. If you find you've got some limiting beliefs, use the following questions to help you update them.

FURTHER THOUGHTS

- If you uncover a limiting belief around feedback, ask yourself how holding this belief helps you. *Example:* As a leader, if Dee believes feedback is a complete waste of time, she doesn't have to have feedback meetings with her team so she saves herself time. If the feedback isn't all positive for her members, she also avoids confrontation, which she's very happy to do.
- What's a more empowering belief to hold instead?

> Instead of believing feedback is a waste of time, Dee can upgrade that belief to seeing it as a way to support her team's development. She could also see it as a way to support her own leadership development.

- What are three things that you feel are important in delivering feedback? Some of my clients say their relationship with the person delivering the feedback is important, and others have said it's more about remaining professional and not taking things personally.

2. Accept That We All Have Blind Spots

'What do you mean you don't snore? The whole house heard you last night! Trust me, you snore.'

'You say you don't, but every time someone goes to overtake you, you speed up. It's not a race.'

'Are we late for something I don't know about? Slow down, woman, you're not in New York anymore!'

The third one, and only the third one, pertains to me! I definitely don't snore and if you ever saw me driving, you'd understand why the second one isn't mine. But when it comes to walking somewhere, I am a woman on a mission, and I just cannot understand how some people are strolling along on the sidewalk as if they've nowhere to be. The thing is, I don't realise I'm doing it. I'll move at the same pace whether I'm going to meet a friend in Central Park, whether I'm shopping in Dubai Mall, or walking to my granny's at home. It's just who I am.

We all have areas or aspects of behaviour unknown to ourselves that others see perfectly clearly, and it's through feedback that we can learn these things about ourselves. Having greater self-awareness allows us to adjust to the situation better, whether we're sleeping, driving, walking, public speaking, leading, whatever.

Knowing our own blind spots is valuable, but becoming aware of them isn't always easy. It can take great courage to ask for feedback and to be open to it, but it's worth it if we want to do better. Imagine going through life not knowing something about yourself that you do on a regular basis? It's not that this is a bad thing; we simply don't know what we don't know and that includes things about ourselves.

Of course we don't always ask others about our potential blind spots because we might presume they're going to be negative. I notice this particularly when I discuss 360° feedback reports with my clients: They're often surprised to see their colleagues rate them a lot higher than they've evaluated themselves in certain areas or skills: 'I wouldn't say empathy is one of my strengths, Linda, but look at how my team have rated me in that category, wow.' Or, 'All of my direct reports have said I'm emotionally intelligent, but I really don't think I am. Could they all be wrong?'

No, they can't all be wrong. We all have blind spots and they're not all negative.

Take the plunge and ask someone you know and trust about something you feel you don't know very well about yourself. *Example:* I'm doing this self-awareness exercise. How much of a risk-taker/how courageous/how assertive do you think I am?

FURTHER THOUGHTS

- What's something you know to be true about yourself but are learning to be okay with it? I can be incredibly selfish with my time. If I wasn't, I wouldn't get my writing done. That doesn't mean it's not something I keep an eye out for, but I understand it serves a purpose.
- Are there particular areas in your life that you think you might have blind spots about?
- Who could you ask to help you gain that awareness?

3. Check Your Purpose for Providing the Feedback

One of the worst feedback sessions I ever had in my professional career started off with this absolute gem. Get ready for this, it's priceless:

'I had heard such good things about your teaching, so you

can imagine my disappointment when I saw you in action. I mean, the other members of the Senior Leadership Team were always going on about how great you are, well, now I can prove them wrong, eh?'

What. The. Absolute. Hell? For what it's worth, and not that I have to justify myself to anyone here, I was a bloody brilliant teacher. But that's beside the point. More wonderful golden nuggets of this guy's "observations" were peppered throughout the conversation, which I'd also like to add was taking place outside in the blazing Dubai heat. When I suggested we sit inside, he said he needed his daily dose of vitamin D and insisted we stay put—I kid you not. The more I listened to what was being said to me, the more it transpired that the purpose of this conversation wasn't to support my professional growth and development as a teacher, it was so that this "leader" could return to his leadership team and tell them he had now gathered substantial evidence to prove them wrong: I wasn't a great teacher after all.

Unfortunately, this situation isn't that uncommon. Not everyone uses feedback conversations as learning moments or coaching opportunities. Some people might just enjoy hearing the sound of their own voice, to get one up on the other person, to demonstrate status, prove a point, and so on. None of which are about empowering the other person. If there's any hint at all that the feedback conversation is not about the other person's development or improvement, use that as a sign to press pause and get aligned on the purpose before having the conversation. If you find yourself wanting to give feedback about the person and not their behaviour, stop yourself and ask what would be the purpose in doing that?

Remember that this is about awareness and not judgement. If you do find you're out to prove a point or highlight someone else's mistake, park the conversation until you've worked through this yourself.

ACTION STEP

Use an upcoming feedback opportunity as a chance for you to get clear on the purpose of that conversation: How are you seeking to empower the other person as a result?

FURTHER THOUGHTS

Use the following questions to help guide your next feedback conversation:

- What's your ideal outcome, for everyone involved, in this session? When we keep that positive outcome in mind, it can help keep the conversation focused on learning and growth. It can also help us keep emotions in check.
- What, if anything, would you have to adjust about your behaviour to achieve that outcome? Being mindful of our nonverbal communication can make the world of difference, making sure our tone is congruent with the words we're using.

Just Three Ways to Get Your Needs Met in a Relationship

'Are you okay?'

'I'm fine.'

'Really? Because you don't sound fine.'

'I'm fine,' I said snarkily, as I huffed loudly once again, slammed my book (which I had been pretending to read for the last half hour), pursed my lips, and stared blankly at the TV. I knew full well that Steve was staring at me and hoped that this would somehow communicate to him that I desperately want him to apologise for earlier.

'Okay then. Glad you're fine.'

Is he serious? Clearly I'm not fine. Even the tortoises can see I'm not fine, but he can't. What is wrong with him?

'Oh. My. God,' I shouted, throwing my arms in the air and storming out of the room.

Many of us don't know how to get our needs met in our relationships, and I'm a prime example of that right here. I'm a wonderful example of what not to do in terms of wanting the other person to suddenly become a mind reader. Thankfully, I have learned a lot about relationships and communication in general since that incident, and when it comes to making sure that my needs are met in my marriage or indeed in my other close relationships, I use the following three reminders as my golden guidelines.

Quick caveat: Keep in mind that it's not up to your partner to fulfill your needs that you're unwilling to fill for yourself—it can't be double standards. Do you treat yourself the way you'd like your partner to treat you? Do you prioritise yourself the way you'd like to be prioritised in the relationship?

1. Be Assertive

'Isn't that the same as being aggressive, Linda? There's a woman at work who some people describe as being assertive and honestly, I think she's a bit of a bitch.'

'I don't know if I could say that, maybe I'll just see if things change on their own.'

'I've never known how to communicate like this, it's so new for me. I was always told to shut up as a child and I'm embarrassed to say I've taken that into my adult relationships and now that's what I tell my children to do. I was never taught to speak like this.'

And there lie our biggest challenges when we talk about being assertive. It gets thrown in the same bucket as *aggressive* even though it's most definitely not. It often doesn't feel right to be assertive, so we act passively instead and hope the problem will just go away on its own.

When we act aggressively, we're out to have our own needs

met without any regard for the other person. It's about winning, it's forceful, threatening, and disrespectful. Being assertive, on the other hand, is based on making sure that both people's needs are met. It's a positive form of communication built on a foundation of respect that seeks to create a win-win.

Here's how we can do it better:

- Always start with taking responsibility for how you're feeling using "I" statements. For example: 'I feel as if I've not heard when...' 'I feel disrespected when...'
- Avoid "you" statements in the conversation. This is important because as soon as we say "you" the finger of blame pops up straight away and we're no longer taking responsibility for how we're feeling and blaming the other person instead, which isn't helpful.
- State what you want instead of what you're currently getting. That could be: 'I feel disrespected when I get interrupted when I'm speaking. I'd like the time to finish what I'm saying.'
- State how this will help the relationship. For example: 'This will help me feel heard more and when I feel heard I feel valued and I don't feel the need to shut down; I can communicate better with you.'
- Ask for the other person's opinion. It's important that both people are in agreement with the requested change or it's not going to work. That might sound like: 'Can you do this for me?' 'What are your thoughts?' 'What will work best as we move forward?'

(ACTION STEP)

Before you have the big conversation where you want to be assertive, create time to get clear on what you want instead of what you're currently getting in the relationship and what you now need. Without that clarity, you run the risk of delivering a mixed message, which helps no one.

FURTHER THOUGHTS

Being assertive is a skill and as with any skill it can take time. It can feel awkward at first to ask for what you want, especially if you've never done it before or if you haven't known how to do it.

* How do you feel about being assertive?
* In what situations do you feel being more assertive would help you?
* What, if anything, would you need in order to be more assertive in those situations? *Example:* I've got the steps, but I feel I'd need to practice more. I could write out a script for myself to see how it might sound and get familiar with the language I could use.

2. Check the Story You're Telling Yourself

'It's the towels on the bathroom floor. He does it all the time and I mean all the time, it's so frustrating, Linda.'

'What's the story you tell yourself when you see those towels on the bathroom floor, Kate?'

'I tell myself he doesn't care. I tell myself he expects me to pick up after him just like his mother did for so long. I tell myself he doesn't respect me.'

We place meaning on everything, including what happens in our relationships. Based on our own values, beliefs, experiences, background, culture, etc., we create a story in our heads and it's not always a helpful story. Sure, sometimes that story is based on the absolute facts of a situation and other times it's based on assumption. The story also changes depending on how we're feeling. Kate told me that there are days when the towels on the floor just don't bother her. She often picks them up and carries on about her day with a smile on her face. But when she's feeling down, she recognises that she tells herself a very different story about those towels.

The story we tell ourselves is important because it strongly influences how we think, feel, and behave. Our negative stories can trigger strong emotions and naturally produce negative reactions, not logical responses, just as Kate continued to describe.

'I'll go stomping around the house. Keith will then come home and I'll give him the silent treatment, but for what? Because I've convinced myself that when he leaves wet towels on the floor that he's disrespecting me? It's ridiculous now that

I hear myself say it out loud.'

When I asked Kate if she felt disrespected in her relationship with Keith, she confirmed that she didn't. There was something completely different going on with her work where she actually felt she wasn't respecting herself but was projecting that onto Keith.

Before we go believing the story we're telling ourselves, it's so important to take a step back and look at the facts first. But the good thing about stories is that they're just stories, they're not facts. And because they're our stories in our heads, we have the power to change them. We have the power to write new stories all the time, to edit and re-edit as we see fit.

So what we need to do is to scrutinise and question our story. *Is this really true? Do I know for sure that this is the way it is? What are guesses, assumptions, and projections, and what are the actual facts?*

ACTION STEP

Investigate your own story to separate facts from assumptions.

FURTHER THOUGHTS

* *When I don't feel heard in my relationship, the story I tell myself is...*
* *The role that I play in that story is...*
* *The next time I catch myself telling that unhelpful story, I will remind myself...*

3. Be Vulnerable

Don't say it, don't say it to him. Just let it go. Deal with it yourself. Come on. He'll think you're nuts. Just pretend it's fine. Oh God, are you actually going to say it? Here we go. I can't look.

And that part of me that wants to pretend everything is fine looks the other way as I prepare to be vulnerable with Steve.

'Can I talk to you for a minute about something? It might take me some time to get this out because it's hard for me to say it for a number of reasons. What I'd like is for you to just hear me out and then we can chat about it, is that okay?'

'Sure, babe, what's up?'

'I'm still upset about the comments that were made at dinner the other night. I know I said I was okay about it, but I realised I'm not. I know now that I got upset because some stuff around food is coming up for me again and I'm not really sure how to deal with it. I thought it was all over, but there're some things I need to work on. I need your support with this and part of that means not making comments about the amount that I'm eating in front of others. Can you do that for me?'

'Totally. Whatever you need. I'm sorry my comments upset you and I'll do better. I was trying to be funny but I know I wasn't. Now can we have some pizza? All this talk of food has made me hungry.'

I love how he makes me laugh.

It's funny that I avoid being vulnerable so many times with the person closest to me and yet, when I do take that risk, I feel closer to him than ever.

When I first started writing this piece, I immediately noticed the resistance. I could feel myself shy away from my laptop as I tried to type the words, because vulnerability is so scary. It feels icky. I just want it to go away because I feel being vulnerable is the complete antithesis of the person I want to be: brave, strong, resilient. But not vulnerable. It's weak to be vulnerable. And when we're weak that's when we can be hurt most easily. So, we protect ourselves and we play it safe. We don't risk saying what we really need in our relationships, and as a result we can end up playing a role in a relationship instead of being our authentic selves.

But as I've just mentioned checking the story we tell ourselves about a partner's behaviour, let's check our vulnerability story while we're at it too; let's separate the facts from the assumptions. Vulnerability guru Brené Brown tells us that vulnerability isn't weak at all. She says, "It's our greatest measure of courage" and when I see it through this lens of courage and bravery, it makes such a difference and fits so beautifully with the person I want to be.

ACTION STEP

If demonstrating vulnerability is completely new for you, ease into it by sharing smaller pieces of information first. Paddle in the shallow end of the pool first before you jump into the deep end.

FURTHER THOUGHTS

+ What's your own vulnerability story? I used to think

vulnerability was a sign of weakness but now see it as a sign of bravery.

- Who do you know who models vulnerability well?
- What could you learn from them about being vulnerable? I learn from my close friends all the time, and I've learned that people usually respond to my vulnerability positively, so it encourages me to demonstrate it more.

Just Three Ways to Deal with Toxic Relationships

W e become like the five people we spend most of our time with, so as you think about the people you spend your time with, ask yourself: Do they motivate, encourage, and support you to become the very best version of yourself? Or do they criticise, judge, and belittle you? One of the healthiest things we can do for ourselves is remove ourselves from toxic relationships. How far you remove yourself is completely up to you—be mindful of the company you keep.

There's a myriad of research done to prove that people who invest in and work at building lasting relationships are happier, less prone to anxiety and depression, have greater self-worth and self-esteem, and find it easier to trust others. There's even some research to show that creating strong relationships can even help us live longer too.

But what about our other relationships, the less positive ones? You know the ones I mean, right? The ones that aren't so good for our mental health; the ones that we know don't increase the longevity of our lives. What do we do about those?

Because let's face it, some relationships are definitely easier to leave than others. Use these three things to identify if you're in a toxic relationship and what you can do about it.

1. Call It What It Is

'He's not possessive, he just really loves me and loves spending time with me. Plus, my friends aren't really his type. Actually, he's suggested I don't spend as much time with Sam anymore. He just prefers when it's just the two of us. I feel so special!'

'She can be quite critical of me. She says she makes these comments to make me stronger, that I'm too sensitive and people walk all over me. I could use a strong woman like her in my life.'

'The latest is that he's asked me to lose a few pounds. He's started pointing out other women to me and saying things like, Have you ever thought of having implants? But honestly, I'm fine with how I look. I look good!'

Signs of a toxic relationship include any form of abuse; being possessive, jealous; constant criticism or judgement; constant negativity; manipulation; attempts to control the other person, their relationships, or money; placing blame on others or lack of accountability for behaviors; disrespect; a lack of consideration for the other person; a "what's in it for me" type of attitude; keeping score; not accepting no as an answer, etc. And make no mistake, the relationship does not need to have this whole combination of behaviours for it to be considered toxic—one is enough.

Yes, every relationship has its ups and downs: I probably

work too much, Steve has a mountain of clothes on his side of the room that will never find their way to a wardrobe or drawer, I don't tidy away used popcorn bags, I've a mountain of empty boxes all over the apartment for some reason, whatever. But that's not the kind of thing I'm talking about. If any of the quotes above rang any bells, or you seem to be making excuses for someone's behaviour and blaming yourself a great deal, ask yourself honestly whether the relationship is doing you any good.

ACTION STEP

Relationships should never cost you your happiness. If you're concerned you might be in a toxic relationship, make time to talk to a trusted friend or professional.

FURTHER THOUGHTS

Not all toxic relationships start off that way, which can make them harder to spot.

- Do you feel heard/valued/respected in this relationship?
- Does your partner ever monitor or control what you do?
- If your best friend was in a similar relationship to you, what would you think/say/do?

2. Explore Ways of Responding

My client Julie was having a really difficult time with her sister and was unsure what to do about it. Part of her valued family so much that she knew she couldn't cut ties with her sister completely, and she had her relationship with her nieces and nephews to think of too. But another part of her was so fed up with the years of belittling comments and nasty behavior that she knew she had to start doing something differently. Anytime Julie spent time with her sister, be it in person or in phone conversations, she came away feeling worse. She was sad about what the relationship had come to, but she also felt disappointed with herself for not knowing how to handle it better and upset for the way she allowed her sister to make her feel. Eventually she decided enough was enough.

Julie knew it was a relationship she had to keep, but now she would be in charge of the way she decided to keep it. As we discussed making new boundaries with her sister, we explored what Julie was okay with and what she was no longer okay with. One change Julie was adamant to make was how she responded to her sister's negative comments. She noticed that whenever they were at a family event, her sister would make disparaging comments about Julie's previous relationships in front of everyone, almost like it was for entertainment purposes. Her sister's husband would laugh, as would some other people. For years, Julie's reaction was the same: just ignore them. She didn't want to make a scene but yet she was bursting to tell her sister where to put her comments. 'I'd sit there, saying nothing, listening to them laugh about my failed relationships, when what I really wanted to do was tell her where to go. I hate saying nothing, I feel powerless.'

For Julie, part of establishing her new boundaries was responding to such comments in a calm and appropriate manner. With a family wedding a few weeks away, she'd have the perfect opportunity. Her sister wouldn't be able to resist trying to embarrass her in front of extended family. Sure enough, as cousins sat around reminiscing, her sister brought up one of her favourite go-to tales about one of Julie's ex-boyfriends who was now gay.

I just loved Julie's response instead of her usual silence: 'You love that story, don't you, Clare? You tell it any chance you can get. Tell me, what's missing in your own relationships that encourages you to bring up my past ones all the time?'

If you have someone like Julie's sister in your life, work on a list of things you're okay with in the relationship and things you're not okay with. How will you assert yourself the next time they do something from the second list?

FURTHER THOUGHTS

- I've often felt in a similar situation to Julie, where I didn't feel completely comfortable in a relationship but also felt I couldn't just leave it. Something that helped me in those situations was to remind myself to be the adult in the room. If the other person wants to mock or belittle me, that's their choice. I'll maintain my composure and remember that I'm the adult there, choosing mature behaviour in a way that works for me.

- What would it look like to "be the adult" for you? *Example:* For me, it was always about standing tall and keeping myself grounded, not shrinking down or trying to hide from the other person.
- What might be different about how you would respond to the other person? *Example:* When I reminded myself to be the adult in those situations, I felt a greater sense of control and instead of feeling the need to beat them at their own game, I often just remained silent.

3. Leaving the Relationship

Isn't it great when toxic people just leave our lives? It's like the trash has taken itself out. I love it!

But unfortunately, toxic people don't always just go away by themselves and there comes a time when we've got to be the ones to cut the cord.

When it comes to leaving a toxic relationship, first and foremost you need to get clear on what you want, otherwise you end up delivering mixed messages and establishing leaky boundaries.

If it's a relationship you want to remove yourself from completely, that's great; just get clear about how that will sound when it's communicated to the other person. I remember being so scared when I eventually built up the courage to leave an incredibly toxic relationship. I feared for my safety and my mental health. It took everything I had at that point, and my best friend's unwavering support, to say to this guy, 'It's over. Don't ever call me again. Don't ever approach me again. I never want to see you again. It's over.'

Once you're clear on what you want moving forward, make sure that you've got a strong support system around you. It doesn't matter what that looks like as long as it works for you. It might be one trusted friend, a group of friends, a coach, a mental health professional, a pet, or all of the above. Support is crucial at this time.

Sometimes, we can get sucked back into toxic relationships quite easily, because we feel bad for the other person, we might hear how they're not doing well without us, etc., but that is not your fault. You need to prioritise your own self-care and know that you're not responsible for anyone else. I frequently got sucked back into relationships because I had such low self-esteem and self-worth, but we live and we learn and we certainly get stronger.

ACTION STEP

If you're unclear about the message that you want to deliver to the other person, get all your thoughts out of your head and onto paper and discuss them with a friend. When we're so caught up in something it can be hard to think logically and rationally about it. The prompts below will help with this exercise.

FURTHER THOUGHTS

* *Being in this relationship is no longer good for me because...*
* *What I want moving forward is...*
* *If I feel the urge to go back to this person, I will...*

4

LIFE'S
EVERYDAY
CURVEBALLS

Just Three Ways to Tackle Procrastination

I don't know about you, but I've noticed that my procrastination monkey's time to shine is most definitely when there's a deadline fast approaching for something I find very challenging. Take writing literature reviews as part of my Positive Psychology course, for example. I had never written one before and although I was great at doing all the reading and research (which I found "easy") when it came to putting the assignment together, even ironing started to look very appealing!

Although fear can be a key motivator in many situations, in others, it can cause us to freeze. I procrastinate when the risk of getting something wrong, or not doing well, is high. Some of us struggle to get started on things that we find boring or things that don't really seem that important to us. We might also procrastinate when the potential reward for doing the work seems too far into the future: Our brain thinks there's no need to panic just yet, and lo and behold, the procrastination monkey comes out to play!

Whatever your reason for procrastinating, these three tools have gotten me through many assignments so far, and they'll have you ticking off your own tasks in no time at all too.

1. Know Your Time Thieves

I'll just have a quick look on...
I wonder what's going on with...
Gosh I love these videos of puppies...

Yes, the videos of puppies clambering all over each other will keep us watching for another few minutes, right? And of course, there's always one more video, and there's the click bait, the Instagram inception... and that's just social media. Let me be very clear that I am not the fun police, and I am certainly not talking about taking away things that we might use to relax, disconnect, or unwind at the end of the day—I'm talking about time thieves.

Time thieves are those things that steal our time when we really want to get things done. They're those habits we easily fall into and they're crimes we're probably all guilty of committing, be it in our professional or personal lives. Professionally, time thieves can rob us in the form of scheduling meetings without a clear purpose, they can show up in the form of creating vague goals where people aren't sure what they're working on or toward, and so time thieves disguise themselves in poor communication too.

Time thieves can cheat us out of time we need and want through procrastination; we might put things off because we're unclear about what we want, it might seem too challenging—like me with my literature reviews—or too easy, or we might be caught in the perfection-procrastination-loop (more on this in a minute). Time thieves go on a spree when we say yes to things we really want to say no to, when we attempt to multitask, and when we're disorganised.

Although no one is telling you not to spend time on social media or not to chat with your colleagues, if you recognise these habits as some of your time thieves, it's time to lay down the law with these criminals!

ACTION STEP

Spend some time exploring your own time thieves. What are some of your most popular ones?

FURTHER THOUGHTS

Time thieves easily creep in when we don't have healthy boundaries in place around our own time.

* Where would you love to be more in control of your time thieves?
* How would this help you? *Example:* Maybe you would feel more productive and better about yourself, or maybe it would give you more time to do something you've been putting off for a while.
* What boundaries could you put in place to manage your time thieves better?

2. Check In with Fear

Fear wears many disguises; procrastination is just one of them. Because of this clever disguise, we might not recognise fear immediately. It's only when we stop and ask ourselves what's really holding us back from getting started that we get a glimpse of what's actually going on. We can easily be held back by fear of failure, fear of getting it wrong, fear of being judged by others, fear of not being good enough, fear of being "caught out" or seen as an impostor, and just not realise it. Yes, fear wears many disguises.

Ever since I was a kid I was terrified of getting things wrong, because at some stage I started telling myself the story that if I got things wrong or made mistakes it meant I wasn't good enough. Unfortunately, it was some time before I edited that, so even as an adult I believed that making mistakes reduced my self-worth. When we see how paralyzing fear can be and how frequently it can show up, it's no wonder we procrastinate. It can be our way of protecting ourselves from that fear: The longer I put off starting my assignments, the longer I delay the fear of being evaluated and not being good enough.

Once we recognise that fear is a factor, we can do something about it. We can label the fear so we know what we're working with. We can shine light on the fear and find out whether it's a valid concern or an irrational fear. For example, I might put off making an appointment with the doctor because there's a history of cancer in my family and I'm genuinely scared. A valid concern. On the other hand, I put off making a dentist appointment because I'm afraid she'll tell me all my teeth are falling out—less valid! We can reframe the fearful situation to something more empowering. Instead of being afraid that people will find out what I don't know, I can see this as a chance to learn and expand my skillset.

ACTION STEP

Think/talk/write on how fear holds you back from taking action.

FURTHER THOUGHTS

- When are you most likely to procrastinate?
- How do you usually get yourself out of procrastination mode and into action?
- Procrastination can be a symptom of perfection—perfectionists fear not being able to complete a task "perfectly" so they continuously put it off. If this sounds like something you can relate to, how can you break this perfection, procrastination, paralysis cycle? I'm so familiar with this cycle, and to get myself out of it, I find it really useful to aim for excellence instead of perfection.

3. Reverse Engineer Your Project

Think about an upcoming important task that you have to complete. Maybe it's a task with a number of different aspects to it and one that will take you some time. It could be a personal task or a professional task.

Now, as you think about that task, knowing the importance of it, the time it will take you, and the number of pieces to it, how motivated do you feel about starting that task right now?

Probably not highly!

Why? Because quite often, when we think of "big projects" or "important tasks" our brain starts thinking, *Uh oh, this one's not going to be a walk in the park, is it?* And that's a problem because our brain likes simple and easy. We might start to predict (not always realistically, might I add) the difficulties the "big project" *could* bring. We might start to picture the long working hours, focusing on the things (we think) we'll have to say no to in order to get it done, and before we know it, the reasons not to start the project today come flooding in and we're procrastinating happily.

One way to get more productive when it comes to bigger projects is to reverse engineer the work. This simply means that you start with an end goal in mind and work backward, chunking down the tasks, until you have that simple and easy (that your brain loves) first step that you can take right now to get started.

Here's how it might work:

End goal: Have completed manuscript ready to send to my editor, Thalia, by May 30

To get that done, what would I have to do first? I'd have to get the last ten chapters done in the next week (even writing this I can feel my own brain say, *No, no, no!* because it seems like a "big task". This tells me I need to chunk down further to find my first step.)

To get that done, what would I have to do first? Realistically, I can write two chapters a day. (My brain doesn't like the sound of this at all, so this is not my starting point.)

To get that done, what would I have to do first? Before I write the chapters, I need a really clear outline of each one, so I know exactly what I'm writing about. (Still feels like too much work to begin with, so I'll keep chunking down.)

To get that done, what would I have to do first? I would need to write five outlines today and five tomorrow to meet that deadline. (To me, this seems a lot more doable, so this is my starting point. You keep chunking down until you reach the step where your brain goes, *Yup, you can do this, this is easy.*)

To get that done, what would I have to do first? Put my phone away, get a glass of water, and start typing.

ACTION STEP

Choose a project you've been putting off and take yourself through the reverse engineering steps above to find your starting point.

FURTHER THOUGHTS

Once you've chunked down and reverse engineered your project, you'll notice that you've also created a plan to help you move forward. I know that once I have the outlines done, the ideas will come to me much more easily.

Just Three Ways to Manage Uncomfortable Emotions

'I get so f**king angry sometimes, Linda. I get so angry that I just explode into this rage and it's like everyone around me gets sucked into it. Then I can't get myself out of it.'

'I'm consumed by the guilt, you'll get that, you're Irish. Why do they teach you about the fear of God in those Catholic schools but never about how to deal with the guilt?'

'I'm sad. I spend so much of my time sweeping that sadness under the carpet and pretending to be happy and you know what, Linda? It's exhausting. I'm exhausted from it. It needs to stop now.'

The quotes are all from clients, but they could easily be my own. The anger, the guilt, the sadness—I could write another book on those three emotions alone. I was angry about all the pain I experienced. I felt guilty because of the way I treated people and my body during my eating disorder, and I felt overwhelming sadness at not feeling understood. And let's throw shame in there too for good measure, because I'm ashamed to say that although I'm just forty now, it's only in the last few years that I've really learned to manage these uncomfortable emotions better. But as one of my clients said above, they don't teach you these things in school, and we don't know what we don't know.

We need to learn how to manage uncomfortable emotions for our own mental well-being. It's not bad or wrong to feel anger, sadness, guilt, or any other emotion—we have emotions for a reason. The trouble starts when we don't process the emotions effectively, when we try and stuff them down or numb ourselves. Although we might think we're protecting ourselves in some way by not talking about these emotions, we're actually doing ourselves more harm than good because silence can breed shame. Before I had the following three tools in my self-management toolkit, my go-to tool was to shut down and say nothing about how I was feeling—a highly ineffective tool, I'd like to add. I don't recommend it! Here's what I do recommend:

1. Explore Them

I love the word *explore*. It's just great. It hasn't got the negative connotation that *judging* has; rather, it's about looking, learning, discovering, and being curious, which is exactly what we want to do with emotions. Park that judgement and just get curious.

We can start to explore emotions by first doing our best to label them. When you notice something triggered inside you, do your best to name it because then you know what you're dealing with. It's not a quiz show, so it's never about getting it "right" first time, it's simply about exploring. When I tried this first and asked myself, *What am I experiencing right now?*

I honestly didn't have the vocabulary to pinpoint what I was feeling. I just kept getting an automatic response of, *I'm so mad.* I knew there was more to it and I knew I wasn't mad in every situation where I was triggered, so I started researching emotions. Being able to pinpoint and differentiate between feeling disgusted, excluded, or disrespected is incredibly empowering and helps us identify what's needed instead.

ACTION STEP

Once you've labeled the emotion experienced, rate it on an intensity scale from zero to ten. This will help you identify certain situations where you might feel particularly triggered, allowing you to adapt to or even avoid such situations in the future.

FURTHER THOUGHTS

Explore your emotions with curiosity and explore them with kindness. *Example:* Once I've identified that I'm feeling disrespected, the last thing I need is to start beating myself up for that. Showing myself kindness and respect will go a lot further.

- When was the last time you felt angry/sad/guilty?
- What was it that triggered that emotion?
- How did you manage it at the time?

2. Validate Them

It's important to remember that when we talk about validating someone else's emotions, it's not about putting that person's needs before our own, nor is it about agreeing completely with the emotion that's expressed or believing that it's warranted in that situation. Validating emotions means that we accept the other person's emotions, knowing they have a right to feel whatever emotion they want. We're acknowledging their reality. We express that acceptance and do our best to understand it. Sure, we might struggle to understand how a particular emotional response has shown up in a certain context, but when it comes to other people's emotions we never have any right to tell someone else how they *should* feel in any given situation.

When we invalidate emotions, people can feel ignored and dismissed. It seriously damages relationships. It causes pain, leaves the other person feeling unheard, not important or valued in the relationship. It can sound like this:

'You're not really feeling that way.' / 'That's ridiculous to feel that way.'

'What is wrong with you?' / 'Pull yourself together.'

'How could you still be hungry/tired/upset/sad?'

By validating the emotions of others we're showing we respect that person and their own experience; it's a fundamental aspect of a healthy, caring relationship. It can sound like this:

'I'm here for you.'

'I hear you.'/ 'I hear your frustration.'/ 'I hear your pain.'

'I can understand why you'd feel like this, this is such a difficult situation.'

We can see why it's so important to validate others'

emotions, and because double standards are as useful as a chocolate coffeepot, if it's important for our relationships with others, it's important for our relationship with ourselves too. Validating our own emotions is about recognising what comes up for us in certain situations and doing our best to be aware of that. It's about noticing this real response, not judging or criticising, just noticing. All of our emotions contain valuable information about ourselves, and if we continually dismiss them, we do ourselves a complete disservice and miss out on valuable self-awareness. If I'm sad but I continually tell myself to snap out of it because I've no reason to be sad, what good does that do? What's the message I'm giving myself with that instruction? That it's not okay to be sad, or that I need to be happy all the time? That's not healthy.

ACTION STEP

Accept your emotions when they come up, knowing they've shown up for some purpose. Ask yourself, *What can I learn about myself here? What can this emotion teach me?* Example: If I feel sad when a friend cancels our lunch date at the last minute, maybe that just means that I value this friendship a lot—that's okay.

FURTHER THOUGHTS

- One reason why we can get uncomfortable with certain

emotions is because we don't know what to say, but remember that there's nothing wrong in admitting that. *Example:* 'While I can't imagine what this is like for you right now, and I'm not sure what to say, know that I'm here for you, what can I do?'

- We might also get uncomfortable with certain emotions because we've suppressed them in ourselves for so long, and when we see someone experiencing that emotion we avoid it for fear of what might come up for ourselves.
- What uncomfortable emotions are you not very comfortable with?

3. The Shadow Side of Gratitude

Did she make a mistake here?
   Gratitude has a shadow side? How?!
   But all the gurus say to do it!
   During the pandemic I started a diploma in Positive Psychology and fell in love with it immediately. And because Gratitude is one of my signature strengths (according to the Values in Action survey) and something I practice every morning, I quickly found myself fully immersed in gratitude for my first assignment. Although I was aware from previous coaching courses that all our strengths have a shadow side, I was unsure how this could apply to something so powerful and joyful as gratitude. How could that practice, which the most successful people in the world swear by, have a shadow side? Well it does.

Here's how gratitude can in fact be toxic.

'Sure, it could always be worse.'
Growing up in Ireland, if you heard this phrase once, you heard it a thousand times. Now, although it's a great reminder to help us keep things in perspective and not catastrophise certain events, how does it help us manage more uncomfortable emotions? How does it help us admit sadness, for example, and deal with it appropriately instead of sweeping it under the carpet? It doesn't, and that's part of the shadow side of gratitude—that it's some sort of panacea.

'Well, at least...'
Then there's the *at leasts*, those two little words that almost act as some kind of a detour from what you were feeling. Your house just burned down? Well, at least you have your health so be grateful for that. But hang on, my house just burned down, I've lost everything! Can I not just wallow in that for a minute? No, no, you have your health, be grateful for that, come on now. Toxic gratitude.

We don't have to look very far to find someone who's having a worse time of it than we are, but that doesn't mean that what we're experiencing or feeling isn't valid. If you're sad, you're sad, that's it; it's valid. You don't have to snap out of it just because someone is having a worse time of it than you are.

It's no wonder so many of us battle mental health issues when we don't think it's okay to talk about the uncomfortable emotions as well as the comfortable ones. We've got to talk about these things more, we've got to accept that gratitude isn't a cure-all. Of course, when we're ready to move on from discomfort, gratitude is a wonderful step to take, but until someone (including ourselves) is ready to do that, let's be more respectful, understanding, and accepting of the experience.

If you're not feeling okay today, I am sorry to hear that. Remember that your feelings are valid; it's okay to not be okay.

ACTION STEP

Don't dismiss your emotions or an uncomfortable experience because you feel you *shouldn't* complain. Carve out some time to write/journal/think or talk about the emotion instead.

FURTHER THOUGHTS

- I can be quick to tell myself, *It could be worse/at least I have...* when...
- Catch yourself the next time you go to reply to someone's negative/uncomfortable situation with *at least*. What would be a more compassionate reply?
- How could you apply that compassion to yourself when you're in a similar situation?

Just Three Ways to
Manage Stress Better

W here do I even start with all of this? Do I need to do all these things because I honestly do not have time for journaling, meditating, having a bath...

Seeking stress management tools can be stressful in itself, which is why I've made this section your one-stop shop to managing stress.

To add to the irony, I was extremely stressed when I wrote this section. But that's a good thing because you know now there are no double standards with me: If my advice is good enough to pass on to you then it's good enough for me to use myself. And I most certainly used these three tools repeatedly to help me get out of the mess, manage myself better, and get sh*t done. Stop your own search for stress-busting tools, don't fill that bath just yet, and tuck into these three things instead.

Let me set the scene—the camping scene, that is. Steve and I arrived in Colorado to start the holiday he had been planning for weeks. He was so excited. We had two weeks of exploring national and state parks to look forward to. Not a hotel in sight, but all the camping space you can imagine. Oh goodie! At the start of the trip I had a call with my fabulous editor, Thalia, and we agreed my full edits would be done in two weeks. *Two weeks? Not a problem. I have all the time in the world.* Two minutes after the call it hit me. *Two weeks to get all my edits done while I'm travelling and bloody camping? No worries!* I convinced myself, *I can do this.* So, while Steve put up the tent, I was searching for plug sockets to charge my laptop.

From my years of experience with stress, I know that a little bit of it can be helpful in spurring me to get moving. But that stress was no longer helpful when I couldn't seem to figure "simple" things out, like what food we needed to buy in the grocery store for our camp dinner that night. I was no longer in control. I was no longer telling myself I could do this. I was properly and completely stressed about meeting my deadline.

1. Establish and Respect Your Own Boundaries

Your boss wants you to work this weekend.

You're at an event and someone makes a remark you feel is completely inappropriate.

You're on a date with someone and you begin to feel uncomfortable.

How many, if any, of the three situations above would have crossed your personal boundaries?

Having clear boundaries is not only a fantastic way to avoid stress, it's also essential for our overall well-being. When we don't have clear boundaries we can easily find ourselves saying yes to things we'd prefer to say no to.

Establishing and respecting healthy boundaries isn't just about knowing when to say no to something at work, it's about knowing what you're okay and not okay with in general.

Boundaries include:

Physical boundaries: e.g., looking after your own physical needs, respecting personal space, how we physically interact with others.

Emotional/mental boundaries: e.g., respecting feelings, the desire to keep information private, making assumptions about how others are feeling, respecting beliefs, values, and opinions.

Material boundaries: e.g., understanding and respectfully abiding by how others feel about lending items and returning them.

Sexual boundaries: e.g., always asking for consent and respecting the reply, not pressuring or making the other person feel guilty for not engaging in sexual activity.

Time boundaries: e.g., respecting other people's time and your own.

How do you know when someone has crossed your boundaries? You get that uncomfortable feeling, sometimes in your gut, that something just isn't right. That's your gut telling you to do something different.

What do you do? When someone crosses our boundaries it's imperative that we stay true to ourselves or we end up feeling more uncomfortable and more stressed. Voice your discomfort or uneasiness about the situation, taking ownership of how you're feeling, knowing that your feelings are valid. Although it might feel odd to do this at first, you're establishing your boundaries, you're showing respect for yourself, and that's always a priority.

'Your comments about my appearance are hurtful, please stop them.'
'I spend Saturdays with my family.'
'I can't do this for you anymore because I need you to learn it yourself.'

Personally, during this editing process, establishing and respecting my own time boundaries was a huge help in reducing the stress I experienced. I told Steve I needed two hours of uninterrupted writing time every day, I rescheduled or cancelled some 1:1 coaching sessions, and I didn't reply to personal messages or emails until I was happy to do so.

ACTION STEP

When establishing your own boundaries, follow the 3Cs of keeping them clear, concise, and having consequences. *Example:* I have a policy of not working after 7 p.m. because that's family time.

- Fear of rejection or guilt can prevent us establishing healthy boundaries for ourselves, but when we fail to set boundaries, we are not respecting ourselves.
- Where, if anywhere, do you allow fear or guilt to prevent you setting boundaries in place? *Example:* I'm a people-pleaser and so I have a natural tendency to say yes to every request. I now pause and ask myself, *Is this something I want to do?* If it is, I will see where I have the time to do it.
- How do you usually handle people invading your personal space? Do you stay there, feeling very uncomfortable with the other person being so close to you? Maybe you step back without saying anything, or maybe you punctuate that step back with a verbal or nonverbal response?

2. Control the Controllable

I cannot stress—no pun intended—how important controlling the controllable is when it comes to managing our stress better. These three little words—control the controllable—are my life savers and no, I'm not exaggerating. Because we love to be in control, don't we? It makes us feel safe, secure, empowered, all those great feelings, so it's no wonder we look to establish control where we can.

And although saying control the controllable might sound

like common sense, how many of us actually do it? Here's how I used this tool during my editing stress marathon:

Grab a pen/pencil and a piece of paper.

Write down the stressor at the top of your page—I wrote "time to meet editing deadline"—and draw two columns underneath that title. Label column one with: Things I cannot control about this, and label column two with: Things I can control about this.

In column one, list the things you cannot control about your current stressful situation. I wrote down: the deadline, the fact that I'm camping and not in the comfort of my apartment, Wi-Fi connection in the campgrounds, my laptop just decided it wouldn't work one day, a local Starbucks Wi-Fi connection being down on another day. It's all happening on this trip.

Although it can feel disheartening to see the things you cannot control on your piece of paper, bear with me.

Once you've created that list, move on to column two. Starting with you—because that's something you always have 100 percent control over—list the things you can control about the stressor. Make this list as long and as specific as you possibly can, noticing how empowering it is to add to this list. I wrote down: how I speak to myself, how I treat myself, how I communicate with Steve, how I use the time I have available, how I communicate with Thalia, worst case scenario I can return to New York if I really need to.

Here's your final step: As you look at the two lists you've just created, take the list of things you can't control and tear it up. That's right, tear it up! It's useless to you anyway because you can't do anything about those things, so why hold on to them or why put any more time and energy into them?

After being away for ten days and consumed by stress for

most of that time, I turned to Steve and told him I needed to go back to New York to meet my deadline successfully. And I did. Always seek to control the controllable.

Be as specific as you can when you're making your list of all the things you can control about the stressor, because it's way more empowering. Consider your thoughts about the stressor, actions you can take, and list them all—how you talk about the stressor, how you view the stressor, etc.

FURTHER THOUGHTS

- Don't just skim your list. Really read it and really step into the state of being in control.
- Knowing that deep breathing can be powerful in helping you regain control, imagine you're inhaling confidence with every breath and letting go of all that stress as you exhale. You might even read through your list whilst in your power pose!

3. Edit Your Explanatory Style

'This is just who I am, Linda, I'm a stressy person.'
　　'What does that even mean, Hamad?'

'I get stressed easily. There's *always* a lot of stress in my life, there always has been, and there always will be. I have to accept that. My job is stressful, my homelife is stressful—life is just stressful, Linda.'

What do you notice about the way my client Hamad talks about stress?

First of all, he makes it part of who he is, so it's personal. Then Hamad tells us how permanent stress is in his life. Finally, he tells us that the stress he experiences isn't just contained to one or two areas of his life, but it's life in general that's stressful, so for Hamad, stress is pervasive.

Identifying the sources of our stress—the stressors—is key to managing stress. It can be easy to pinpoint a particular part of our job, moving house, or a relationship as the source of stress, but what if we are the source of our stress, specifically the way we explain our stress? Our explanatory style can easily exacerbate stressful situations when we describe them just as Hamad did: personal, permanent, and pervasive, because it makes us feel helpless and powerless to create change.

If that is the case, we need to edit our explanatory style of stress. We need to make sure it's no longer personal, pervasive, and permanent, but more external, temporary, and specific. Here's how it worked with Hamad: First, he stopped making stress so personal and associating it with his personality and started talking about stress as an external factor, which made him feel less helpless almost immediately. Second, Hamad stopped assigning stress a permanent role, as something that's "always" there to something that's temporary and will pass. Third, he stopped explaining stress as something that affects all areas of his life to recognising that it's actually specific to his work, usually at a particular time of the year. As he said himself at the end of our coaching session one day, 'My job can be stressful at times, specifically toward the end of the financial year, but it passes and I learn to manage it better each time.'

Analyse your explanatory style around stress, changing the personal, permanent, pervasive components of it to things that are more external, temporary, and specific.

FURTHER THOUGHTS

- Hamad's explanatory style at the start of our work together was typically pessimistic, where he thought it was all his fault (*just who I am*) and that the problem was fixed (*there always will be stress*). This style of thinking can be pervasive and influence other areas of our life.
- Where else in your life might you be attributing/identifying part of your personality as the root cause of the problem? *Example:* They'd never hire someone like me in a company like that!
- What other problems do you see as being fixed or permanent? *Example:* I'll never meet the right person; there must be something wrong with me.

Just Three Ways to
Navigate Change

'I'm going to Saudi for a teaching job,' I announced to my
father one Sunday over dinner.
'I'll tell you this, Linda, you're not going to Saudi,' my
father replied sternly.
'Dad!'
'Linda!'
'Look, Dad, it's like this. I can't get a teaching job here and
there are hundreds in Saudi. If I don't go, it means I'll end up
living here with you and Mum for God knows how long and
you'll probably have to support me financially too.'
'Right, love,' said my father without any hesitation, "I'll get
your suitcases down from the attic for you.'
And that was it. Having never even set foot in a Middle
Eastern country, I was moving continents to teach English and
Social Studies for a year. In the end, I went to Qatar, a country
that neighbours Saudi Arabia.
I'll never forget the first night I arrived in the Middle East,

and I honestly don't think my roommates will forget the first day they met me either, because I was a bubbling mess! I cried for the entire first week, wondering what the hell I had just done and struggling to cope with the plethora of changes I was faced with. But I obviously survived because I ended up staying in the region for fourteen years when I originally didn't think I'd last fourteen days!

Change is the one constant in life, and it can bring with it a whole rollercoaster of emotions. We might be excited by the prospect of what awaits us on the other side and yet grief-stricken at having to say goodbye to what we know or what we have to let go. Change rocks certainty, messes with familiarity, and can leave us feeling unsafe and unsecure. It's not surprising then that so many of us fear change. But by understanding that fear, learning to let go and getting comfortable with being even a little uncomfortable, we can empower ourselves to navigate periods of change better.

1. Understanding Your Fear Around the Change

Change breeds fear because we don't know what the future holds. As I sat on that flight to Qatar, I had no idea what awaited me on the other side and I was absolutely terrified.

Remember that our brains like simplicity, predictability, and routine. Change doesn't bring any of these things. Change brings a lack of control, unpredictability, the fear of failure, fear of pain, humiliation... I'm really selling it here, aren't I?!

One way we can start to navigate change better is to understand our fears around change. By identifying what frightens us, we can do something about the fear instead of it being like a monster that lurks in the dark. What we can be quick to forget is that all emotions (yes, all emotions) are useful in some context. Fear can encourage us to take action, it can keep us alert, and it can protect us. Fear is information and information is power.

But sometimes our minds get it wrong, and what it might label as fear doesn't necessarily mean there's something to be afraid of. I might be afraid of public speaking in case I make a mistake, but if I live in fear of making mistakes, what will I ever accomplish? Why not shine the light on fear and see what it's all about?

ACTION STEP

Remember that feelings aren't facts, so check the facts of the situation by asking yourself if they are based on reality or are assumptions you're making?

FURTHER THOUGHTS

Having awareness of our fears is empowering because we can take steps to work through them. *Example:* I was afraid of moving to the Middle East because of all the assumptions I made about not being able to handle the change. The reality was that I was more than capable of handling those changes.

- ◆ What assumptions are you making about yourself being able to handle change?
- ◆ What assumptions are you making about the situation or change itself?
- ◆ What's true about your ability to handle change?

2. Letting Go to Let Be

Along with the fear of uncertainty, something else that prevents us embracing the process of change is our focus on what we perceive we may potentially lose, have to give up, or sacrifice as part of that change.

As we navigate through a period of change, we may find that there are certain things we simply won't have as we move forward to our new beginning. This can bring about a deep sense of loss, and there is a process of grieving that needs to be done in order for us to move forward. Although this part of the process may seem like we have no control, we can empower ourselves by accepting our new situation and choosing what to let go of instead of desperately trying to cling to.

It can be helpful to identify what we feel we're losing, and, just like fear, by identifying and naming it, we're in a much stronger position to do something about it. The following are common losses we might experience in a period of change:

- Loss of connection. *Example: How will I maintain my relationships?*
- Loss of security. *Example: How will I provide for my family?*
- Loss of a sense of identity. *Example: If I don't do this job, who am I?*
- Loss of control. *Example: This is being done to me.*
- Loss of confidence or self-worth. *Example: What will others think?*
- Loss of routine/familiarity. *Example: What will I do with my time now?*

Looking at a period of change through a lens of loss is not going to make you feel better or empower you in any way. What will help is acknowledging your sense of loss and allowing those emotions to surface without any judgement at all. There's no point in trying to sweep those emotions under the carpet and pretend they're not there because they'll just show up in another way.

ACTION STEP

Explore uncomfortable emotions from a place of curiosity. Catch any of those *shoulds* that you start telling yourself and break that cycle by responding to yourself with kindness and compassion. Allow things to just be until you're ready to move forward.

- If you're experiencing a period of change right now, what would you benefit from letting go of in order to move forward? *Example:* Letting go of the belief that it *should* be easier/better/more fair.
- What can you learn about yourself from the emotions that are showing up? *Example:* The sadness of leaving good friends can help us realise just how important connections are to us. It can encourage us to look at new and different ways of keeping in touch. It might even help us share our feelings with others more openly.

3. Notice How Resourceful You Are

When anxiety around change creeps in, our ability to manage ourselves and remember how resourceful we are can quickly go out the window. Instead of focusing on the uncertainty of the change, how would it be if you focused on the resources you have at your disposal during this period?

- **Our thoughts:** We always have a choice in the type of thoughts we allow to consume our headspace. When we catch ourselves falling into negative thinking traps about change such as Future Predicting (e.g., *This is all going to go badly*) or Unrealistic Expectations (e.g., *I shouldn't be getting so flustered by this move, it's ridiculous*) we can change these thoughts to something more empowering and constructive (*I'll deal with any challenges if and when they arise*) or (*Moving can be challenging and it's okay to feel flustered right now.*)

- **People:** So you don't have the answers to your questions about this period of change, but maybe someone else does. Who do you know who's been through something similar? Is there an online forum where you could get ideas, tips, and suggestions to make the change go more smoothly?

- **Time:** Time is an incredibly valuable resource to access when navigating change. We can use it to press pause to give ourselves a break, or use it to speed up and take that action we've been putting off. We can ask ourselves, *What can I do to make this easier for myself right now?*

- **Skills:** Whether it's deep breathing (or another breathing technique you use), using a mindfulness practice, visualization, parking a fear to deal with it later, decompartmentalizing... these are all skills and resources. As you navigate this change, what skills do you possess to make it easier for you?

ACTION STEP

Along with the resources just mentioned, resources also include our knowledge, lessons learned from previous experiences, characteristics—literally anything that has helped us overcome a challenge. Use these examples to create a list of all the resources you possess to navigate this change.

FURTHER THOUGHTS

Many of us possess strengths that we forget to leverage in times of change. Could navigating this period call for you to be more patient or assertive? Maybe it calls for you to take a step back, or to step forward and lead?

- How could you demonstrate these strengths right now?
- How would this benefit you and those around you?

5

WHEN THE GOING GETS TOUGH

Just Three Ways to
Reduce Overwhelm

O n Saturday November 7, 2020, our street in Brook-
lyn and the neighbouring streets turned into one huge
block party as people celebrated the victory of Joe
Biden becoming the 46th President of the United States. The
only person not celebrating was me. Was it because I'm the
biggest Donald Trump fan the world has ever known? Most
definitely not! I wasn't celebrating because I was completely and
utterly overwhelmed trying to meet deadlines for our recently
launched well-being app, Upstrive.

I'd been sitting at my laptop since 5 a.m. that morning,
wondering how the hell I was going to get all the work done
in time for a big meeting we had with an educational company
in Saudi the following day. By 11 a.m., I was crying at my desk,
telling myself I wasn't going to get it all done, my sobs being
drowned out by the cheers of jubilation outside on the street.
By 2 p.m. I was fit to throw my laptop out the window and
hand over the well-being app to some of the Joe supporters still
on the streets! But by 3 p.m. I was suddenly making progress,

telling myself I would be done by 5 p.m.—and I was.

It's incredibly hard to function properly when we're over-whelmed. It feels like our thoughts are just spinning instead of flowing in a logical format, our bodies usually following suit, spinning from task to task while we tell ourselves we don't have enough time, and to top it all off, the what-if machine is constantly churning out worrying thoughts about everything that could go wrong. On that Saturday, the following three things helped me survive my overwhelm, and I know they'll help you too.

1. Stop Operating From a Space of Lack

I don't have enough time to do this.

I don't have the mental bandwidth for this.

I don't have, I don't have, I don't have...

Imagine you have a to-do list, List A, and it's just the best to-do list in the world. List A is fantastic because when you look down through the items, no matter how many there are, it doesn't bother you. You're confident you can complete them all and you have all the time in the world to do so; there are no deadlines. When we look at List A, we don't feel overwhelmed or pressured; we feel calm, competent, and confident because we know it's all so doable.

Then there's List B. Although List B is similar because it contains the same tasks, it is incredibly different because it's time-sensitive—very time-sensitive. Isn't it funny that as soon as we know we've tight deadlines to make, we suddenly start thinking of all the reasons we can't do it. We start to focus on what we don't have, and straightaway we're operating from a place of lack.

Looking at any task or project through a lens of lack is an easy way to trigger overwhelm. To change that perspective, we need to be aware of the space we're operating in and check how conducive that is to accomplishing our task. Thoughts of not having enough time will only spur thoughts of not having enough of something else too, which is not helpful.

Catch yourself when you recognise you're coming to a situation or challenge from a place of lack and change your focus. Yes, the reality might be that the time constraints are too tight for what needs to be accomplished, but focusing on that never helps.

(ACTION STEP)

Tell yourself you will do what you can with the resources you have and then start with even the smallest first step.

FURTHER THOUGHTS

♦ Mindset matters: We need to truly believe the positive thoughts we're telling ourselves and act accordingly to get the results we want. Faced with the deadline that day, I stopped thinking, *I don't have enough time*, and started believing, *I have all the time I need.*

- I'm quick to tell myself, *I don't have enough time*, when...
- The next time I catch myself saying, *I don't have enough time*, I will tell myself...
- One way that I've shown the world I'm a formidable force is by...

2. Dealing with the What-Ifs

What if they ask me something I don't know?

Well I'll tell them I don't know it. There's no shame in not knowing, but pretending to know won't help me. Next.

What if you don't get the job?

Well I don't get the job, nothing I can do about that. I'm giving this interview my best shot but not getting the job is not the end of the world. Next.

I was on my way to an interview for a teaching job one morning when I finally had enough of those stupid thoughts. So, instead of pretending they weren't there, I mentally called them out, lined them up against the wall like a bunch of naughty schoolkids, and gave as good as I got! I went through them one by one, replying to their questions and sending them on their way.

The funny thing was that when I acknowledged the thoughts instead of ignoring them, and when I called them out, that shut them up. It was almost like you could see them shying away, or shrinking down, knowing they'd failed in their mission to start that worry cycle again.

Something else that helps with the what-ifs is replying with a nonchalant, *So, what if?*

What if nobody buys my book?
  So, what if nobody buys my book? I've still written a book! Next!

What if people think I'm stupid?
  So, what if people think I'm stupid? I can't control other people. Next!

Remember, the point of acknowledging and replying is to put the what-if to bed, not to ruminate on it. Replying solves this because it shows the what-if that you've got an answer, you've got a plan B and even a plan C. We want to get control of the what-if, not have it control us.

ACTION STEP

Don't let your own pesky what-ifs generate more overwhelm. Catch them, call them out, and take a positive action step if need be.

FURTHER THOUGHTS

- Acknowledging what-ifs and getting curious about them can help us differentiate between an irrational worry that needs to be told off or a helpful reminder in disguise.
- *What if I forget my speech in front of everyone? Maybe writing a few cue cards will help me prepare a little more.*
- Could your own what-ifs be helpful reminders in disguise?

3. Ground Yourself with Gratitude

This is one of my favourite go-to tools in overwhelming situations because it breaks the cycle of spinning thoughts, which naturally helps us choose more constructive thoughts. Gratitude encourages a little bit of mindfulness, which helps bring us back to the present instead of pacing around in the past or racing into the future, and it brings a sense of calm, which helps us move through the overwhelm.

When you catch yourself caught up in the overwhelm, ask yourself, *What are just three things I can see right now that I'm grateful for?* For example, the desk I have to sit at, the hands I have to type with, and the photos on the bookshelf beside me that remind me of family and friends.

Next, ask yourself, *What are just three things I can touch right now that I'm grateful for?* For example, the laptop I have to work on, the legs I have to move with, and my "I love NYC" mug filled with fresh coffee.

Then ask yourself, *What are just three things I can hear right now that I'm grateful for?* For example, the people cheering on the street means there's a political change taking place, the tortoises eating their food behind me as I type (totally obsessed with those little animals), Steve on the phone next door sharing good news with friends.

You could stretch the exercise further and ask: *What are just three things I can smell right now that I'm grateful for?* For example, the perfume I'm wearing always reminds me of our wedding day, the candle on the windowsill because I'm always grateful when I get a good bargain, and the smell of fresh coffee in my awesome mug.

And finally, *What are just three things I can taste right now that I'm grateful for?* For example, the cold water sitting on my desk, the fresh strawberries Steve bought this morning, last night's leftover veggie curry.

ACTION STEP

If you're not used to it, practicing mindfulness can feel a little odd or awkward, and that's fine. If this particular technique doesn't help ground you, challenge yourself to come up with one that does.

FURTHER THOUGHTS

Don't wait until you're overwhelmed to use this simple and effective tool; it's a great way to manage your state if you feel anxious. And for those of you with children, this is a fantastic technique to teach them too.

Just Three Things to Consider When Making Big Decisions

'**W**hich ones should we get?'
Does this guy I have been married to for over eleven years even know that I've a deadline to meet and that I have not got the mental capacity to think about what he wants to sleep on?

'I can't make a decision about bedsheets right now. I'm trying to decide which chapters to delete from my book. I've too many!'

'Babe, I think the colour of our bedsheets is just as important as this book you've been writing for the past four years now.'

Steve may have had a point, because if he ends up buying the wrong ones, he'll never hear the end of it from me!

Joking aside, if there's anything that just really throws me out of sync, it's making decisions. I absolutely hate it. I hate the pressure, sometimes I hate the choice—but I also complain when I don't have choice. I hate the constant questions and what-ifs that set up camp in my little head, but most of all I hate the fear. I hate the fear of getting it wrong. When it comes to making big decisions, I have always been absolutely terrified of getting it wrong. Why? Because if I get it wrong, it means I've made a mistake and that would mean I'm not perfect. And if there's just one thing you know about me at this stage, it's that I struggled with perfection for years of my life... and sometimes still do.

As a newly qualified teacher, I struggled to decide whether to take a part-time job in a great school in Ireland or a full-time job in London. The decision tormented me for days until I had to give one perspective employer my answer, but even then it didn't feel right and unfortunately I ignored my gut feeling. I struggled to make decisions about staying in the Middle East or moving back home to Ireland, because of a fear of missing out on making good money and fear of judgement from others. I really struggled with the decision to accept a part-time teaching job when my coaching business wasn't going as well as I had hoped it would, for fear of missing out on coaching opportunities and again, fear of what other people would think of my decision. It was in making that big decision, and in plenty of others since then, that I came to trust the following three tools in helping me make the best choice for myself. They work and they'll help you make big decisions too.

1. Check in with Your Three Brains

Some decisions you can make purely on rationale and logic. Some decisions you can make purely on emotion. And some decisions you can make based on intuition alone.

Then there are those decisions that require more—a lot more. There are those decisions that require you to check in with your head, heart, and gut to come to an answer. Some people refer to the head, heart, and gut as our three brains, but whatever you call them, these three decision-makers need to be in agreement in order for us to make those *big* decisions.

Phrases like, "My gut tells me", "My head says do it", "My heart just wasn't in it", or "Part of me just doesn't feel it's the right thing" aren't things we say off the top of our heads—there is deep meaning in them and they are evidence that part of us is not in sync, that something is "off". Most of us are really attuned to these signals and make the time to check them out and explore them more, but some of us don't. Some of us hope they'll just go away. I think a good rule of thumb here is that if in doubt, check it out. If you're not sure why your heart's not in it, find out. If you're unsure what your gut instinct is trying to tell you, explore what is there.

Even though you might be the most logical and rational person reading this right now, you know that when it comes to making big decisions, yes, you need to listen to your head, but you also need to make sure that your decision is aligned with your values; you need to make sure your decision is true to your heart and that you get the "right feel" in your gut for it.

ACTION STEP

Here's a great exercise to help you with check in with your three brains:

Step 1: Set down three separate markers in a space you're comfortable in. Let the markers represent head, heart, and gut in whatever way works for you. Do your best to simply be curious about what comes up and park that judgement; there's no right or wrong here. Tune in to anything that your body is doing from each space too; you might feel compelled to lean forward or back at some points, or you might stand super still the whole time.

Step 2: Step into the marker that represents your head brain. Then, with your feet firmly and evenly on the ground and your arms hanging loosely by your side, ask yourself, *What does my head say about this decision? What's logical about it? What's rational about it?* Make a note of what comes up; you might want to send yourself a voice message or write a few things down while you're in this space.

Step 3: Step off your head brain marker and clear your mind before stepping into the heart brain marker.

Step 4: Knowing that your heart brain is strongly associated with emotion, values, connection, ask yourself, *How much of my heart is in this decision? What's really important to me* *here? How does this decision/decision A honour my values?*

Step 5: Again, when you're ready, step off your heart brain marker and clear your mind.

Step 6: Knowing that your gut brain is the powerful source of intuition, what does your gut say about this decision/decision A? What's behind that? If fear shows up, check in and see if it's real or imaginary, like a form of protection.

Step 7: Step off the marker when you're ready and notice what came up for you in all three areas.

FURTHER THOUGHTS

When faced with a big decision, creating time and space to explore those parts of you that don't feel in sync can be very powerful. It can help us uncover fears, barriers we've created ourselves, or things we need to acknowledge before being able to move forward to make the decision. This was such a powerful step in helping me make the decision about accepting the part-time teaching job because I had been avoiding acknowledging the fact that I missed seeing so many people every day, I missed the community feeling of being in a school, and working for myself wasn't all I thought it was going to be.

2. Check How Each Choice Meets Your Criteria

'You don't get it! If I take this part-time job then I'm not as independent as I want to be! The whole point of me leaving teaching full time was so I could be independent, and by taking this job I'm not anymore.'

Yes, Little Miss Independent, that's me. I was starting to sound like a broken record to poor Steve as I plagued him with the conflict of my decision making. I was so afraid of not having my independence, but I was also drawn to the financial stability the part-time job would give me. I was torn. And let's be honest here, I needed the money. Business was not going as well as I thought it would. It was good, but I had completely underestimated the money I needed to make each month just to simply live in Dubai. I was starting to become worried about money, and that's not me at all because I've always had my own money—see, independence!

'I think you're missing something really important here.'

I eye-rolled internally as I wondered what Steve was seeing about this situation that I wasn't. I had thought of *everything* about this decision, for God's sake, man! But clearly I hadn't thought of everything because what he said next made perfect sense to me and made my decision there and then.

'You keep thinking that taking this job will make you less independent, but I think it will make you even more. If you take this role, after your first month you'll have enough money to buy your own car. That's massive! We won't have to share a car anymore, you won't have to drop me to school every morning, and we both know how much you hate that journey every day. You're always saying you want to contribute more financially, and taking this job will help you do that. You'll still have time to do what you want, to see your clients, whatever you want to do.'

Oh, he knew me so well. As I listened to Steve's version it was as if beside a checklist in my brain, I could just go tick, tick, tick, tick, tick. Done. I was taking the part-time job at the school. I now saw how it satisfied both my criteria for independence and to have more financial freedom.

Get clear on the criteria you're trying to meet and explore how each of your choices helps you meet those criteria. Start by asking yourself what's important to you and use the questions below to dig deeper.

FURTHER THOUGHTS

From my personal example above, you can see how important independence is to me, and making money is a means of meeting that criterion. Sometimes when we ask ourselves what's important about making a decision, money might come up quite quickly, but it's often a "surface" answer. What we're really driven by is what the money can potentially provide us with. *Example:* freedom, security, peace of mind, etc.

- What's important to me? *Example:* Making my own money.
- And what's important about that? (This question helps you start to dig deeper to identify your higher criteria.) *Example:* So I can do what I want, spend what I want.
- And what's important about that? Independence.
- And what's important about that? It's everything. I place huge importance on my independence, it's just who I am.

3. Face the Facts

'Oh, you're the girl who's moving to New York in a few weeks. Have you been before?'

'Yes, I've been a few times during the summer on holidays. I can't wait to move, so exciting!'

'Eh, well, you do know that it's very different living somewhere compared to visiting it on holiday, right? It gets extremely cold there in the winter, you know. Nothing like you're used to here in Dubai...'

Was this guy for real? Did he honestly think I hadn't thought about the facts in our decision to move to the greatest city on the planet? Shut up!

And as it turns out, he was kind of right! When we found out we were moving to New York City, I got so caught up in the romantic whirlwind of finally being able to live in my dream city that I hadn't really considered all the facts of the move. Yes, I knew it was going to be challenging in some ways and I knew it was going to be expensive, blah, blah, blah, but I guess I'm a hopeless optimistic at heart and the truth is that I just didn't want anything to burst my bubble.

I did the same thing when I married Steve after being engaged for a short period of time: I didn't really think about it too much. I knew I loved him and he loved me, what more did I have to think about? It was only when my mum said to me, 'Just out of curiosity, have you lived together yet?' that I suddenly realised I had no idea what this man I was about to marry was like to live with. We'd been on holidays together— okay, that's another lie; we had been on one trip to Thailand together—but things are kind of different when you live with someone full time compared to a relaxing beach holiday over Christmas. Thankfully, that one turned out okay too.

But ignorance is not always bliss and it's not always helpful to do a Linda on it and just hope for the best. It will serve you better in the long run to remind yourself that knowledge is power and that facing the facts of the decision you're seeking is empowering.

(ACTION STEP)

If you're like me and struggle to see the facts of certain choices, speak with two or three people who you know are logical and rational in their decision-making.

FURTHER THOUGHTS

Sometimes the biggest decisions we have to make are incredibly personal. If this is the case and you're finding it hard to make that decision, journaling on the following questions will help you:

* *Who is involved in this decision I have to make?*
* *How is each person involved affected both positively and negatively?*
* *What's the worst thing that could happen and can I cope with that consequence?*

Just Three Ways to
Become More Resilient

'Hey, Miss, you know that mad run you did at the weekend?'

'Yes, Kylie, I do. It's kinda hard to forget what it's like to run up and down a mountain for ten hours!'

'Sure, Miss. But was that the hardest thing you've ever done in your life? Like, it must have been hard, but was that the hardest thing ever?'

I'm not sure if it was the total exhaustion from having run my first ultra-marathon at the weekend or all the work I was doing on myself around mental health that made me blurt out my answer to my group of Year 11s that morning.

'You know what? It wasn't the hardest thing ever. It was hard, but the hardest thing I've overcome in my life so far has been depression and an eating disorder.'

Silence. Absolute silence for probably the first time in the five years I'd taught them. I looked around and they were all just staring blankly at me. And then the big question came: How did I do it? They were genuinely curious. They had mock exams coming up and really wanted to know how to get through tough times. We started talking about resilience. What it really means to come through the other side of something tough and to have grown as a result. Not just surviving the experience, but using it to help you thrive.

I love resilience. I love everything about the concept, and so when I had a full unit on the topic for my Positive Psychology course recently, I was in my absolute element. I spent eight weeks doing a deep dive into resilience, researching all the different facets. It was fascinating. What I loved most was that when it came to looking at ways of building resilience, all the research included the following three things that I learnt to do in my twenties to help me deal with my own mental health challenges. If you're looking to start thriving in life instead of just surviving, these are for you.

1. Take Action

When the sh*t hits the proverbial fan, the last thing you're going to do is stand around to see if you're going to get hit with it, right? So you move, you take action, and that's exactly what we've got to do when any challenge shows up. Nothing changes if we don't take action. You can have all the positive thoughts you want, but unless you're supporting those thoughts with decisive constructive action steps, what's going to change? Nothing.

For a number of reasons, taking action is a powerful step toward developing greater resilience. Mentally, it helps us feel like we're doing something to move through the adversity, so it gives us a sense of progress, a sense of accomplishment. It might involve speaking to someone about what you're experiencing, connecting with a friend, journaling, going for a walk, reading, researching, learning something and applying it to your situation, whatever appropriate action you can take to start moving forward. I learned so much about mental health as a result of my own experience with it, which turned out to be imperative to my recovery. I started learning about Cognitive Behavioural Therapy and applying what I learned to manage my mind better; challenging negative thoughts and negative self-talk. I developed ways of building up my self-esteem, my self-confidence and self-worth. I learned how to feed my body better, focusing on food as fuel. And even though I knew these were all little steps I was taking one at a time, when I stepped back and saw everything I had learned and the progress I was making as a result, it was such a confidence boost.

Taking action also helps us face our fears as we move through adversity. Fear can keep us quiet, make us play it safe, keep us small. It can be debilitating, even paralysing, which is why taking action is such a powerful antidote. Even the smallest action shows fear that we're standing up to it, that we're facing it head-on. Taking action is a fabulous way to give fear the finger and tell it where to go.

(ACTION STEP)

Is there a small step you could take that would move you toward the life you want but that you keep putting off for some reason?

Keep in mind that taking action is also powerful for quelling those pesky what-if thoughts that can so easily pop up as we navigate adversity.

* What resources do you already possess to help you move forward?
* What, if anything, would you need in order to take that action step you've identified above?
* What are you learning about yourself as you move through this challenge you're experiencing?

2. When the Going Gets Tough, Get Tougher

We are always stronger than we think we are. Always, always, always. It might not feel that way, but then again, feelings aren't facts. The challenge can be how to get tougher, especially when we're already finding things tough. It can be challenging because this is exactly when the pity party loves to show up and remind us how difficult things are for us. But this is an important part of demonstrating resilience: being able to press pause on the pity party playlist and press play on the strength slide show, reminding ourselves of the times we've shown perseverance, grit, determination, etc.

One of the mistakes I used to make in applying this step

was thinking that this had to be about "big" demonstrations of mental strength. In my midtwenties I really didn't think I had overcome anything important enough to be considered tough. I sat in front of my psychiatrist one day staring blankly at her when she said to me, 'Come on, Linda, you strike me as a tough cookie, when have you had to be tough?'

'I've not, really, Doctor, in fact I wouldn't say I'm tough at all.'

'I don't believe you,' she said. 'You told me you used to compete as a rider. Did you ever fall off a horse?'

'Did I ever? My God, more times than I got up!' I laughed.

'So, you still got back up. And were you ever scared on a horse?'

'Yes, lots of times. But I didn't show it. You can't, you've got to show the horse who's in control.'

It took me a few minutes to see what my doctor was doing, but eventually I got it and sat there smirking at her while she laughed at me. Despite the fact that I was young, I had already shown how tough I was in many situations. Whether it was not letting a young horse get the better of me, getting through break-ups with boys I was convinced I was in love with as a teenager, or getting through exams at school, Dr Mahmoud was right—I am a tough cookie.

$$\left(\text{ACTION STEP}\right)$$

Jot down a list of situations where you've been tough and shown strength in any of its forms.

- What does being tough mean to you?
- When have you surprised yourself with how tough/ strong you can be?
- How did it feel to demonstrate such strength?

3. Practice Self-Compassion

'What do you tell your daughter when she experiences a setback? Do you encourage her to continually beat herself up and tell herself that she's stupid and *should* be able to do better?'

'Gosh no, Linda! I'm not a monster! But you're right and actually she noticed it about me the day and said, Mom, you need to kind to yourself.'

'What a wise young girl! I wonder where she learned it?'

Although Neila and I shared a quick joke at her double standards, her struggle to show herself some compassion when she experienced a setback isn't funny, and she's most definitely not alone in it either. So many of us are quick to beat ourselves up when we make a mistake, or to dwell on it for hours or even days on end, and yet we'd never encourage anyone else to do that, would we? So why do we think it's okay to do it to ourselves? The last thing we need when we're finding things tough is an extra portion of tough love, so how about we serve ourselves a healthy helping of self-compassion instead—with the option of seconds too!

Showing self-compassion means showing ourselves

kindness, accepting that we all make mistakes, and knowing that all emotions are valid as we move through the discomfort of overcoming setbacks. It's about giving ourselves a break, recognising our efforts, and speaking words of support to ourselves instead of beating ourselves with that judgmental stick as we shout at ourselves to "just push through".

Being compassionate helps us develop resilience, because it's encouraging to have a helping hand when we fall, it's comforting to know we're not alone in making mistakes and in experiencing negative emotions, and these things give us the confidence to try again and again. We'd all be much braver walking a tightrope knowing there's a safety net under our feet, and that's what self-compassion can be.

Overcoming depression and the eating disorder taught me self-compassion. Up until then, I was too busy criticising myself to be compassionate—it's not exactly top of a perfectionist's to-do list, as you can imagine, because when something goes wrong you just go into self-critical mode as if you're on autopilot. But it's a horrible way to treat yourself and so ironic too, to think that constantly chipping away at your self-worth and self-confidence is going to magically give you the confidence you need to get back up on that horse.

(ACTION STEP)

Make it a priority today to treat yourself as you would your best friend: Speak kindly to yourself, show understanding, validate any uncomfortable emotions, and allow yourself to make mistakes.

FURTHER THOUGHTS

- On a scale of one to ten, with ten being incredibly easy, how easy do you find it to practice self-compassion?
- When do you find it more challenging?
- If you loved yourself fully, how would you treat yourself every day?

Conclusion:
Putting It All Together

There are very few things that sit permanently on my desk, but this book is one of them because it contains all the tips, tools, and techniques that I use myself every single day. And if you're reading this now thinking, *She uses this every day? Really?* let me show you just how often I use these skills on a typical day.

First things first: I get my own day off to a better start by practicing gratitude. Depending on how busy I am, I will read for either ten or twenty minutes with the purpose of learning something. I then ask myself what needs to be different about today and journal on that for a few minutes. If there's something else still on my mind, I write it out, asking myself better questions, knowing the benefits of getting that problem out of my head and onto paper.

Remembering to respond, not react is a daily reminder for me, so much so that I have a Post-it with that phrase stuck to my laptop. Inevitably, there's often a difficult email, request, or conversation that triggers an emotional reaction within me and I need that reminder to respond instead. At some point in the day I may well have to grapple impostor syndrome when coaching my executive clients, along with dealing with my good friend the inner critic before I post on social media—and that's all before lunch!

As I run, I manage those *should*-statements that fill my headspace telling me I should be able to run faster or that I shouldn't have to stop after ten minutes. I hear the critical story I'm telling myself and change it to one of praise, acknowledgement, and appreciation for what my body can do.

As things get added to my to-do list over the course of the day and I feel my body tense up with the thoughts of "all I have to do", I prioritise actions and focus on what I can control right here, right now. I break bigger projects into those manageable bite-size chunks I know I can handle.

I catch, challenge, and change the expectations I have of Steve coming home after a full day of teaching to cook us both dinner. When I scroll through social media and notice the comparative narrative creeping, I pause and compliment both the person on the screen and myself—what a difference that makes.

As I shut my laptop down for the evening and see my book sitting on my desk, I'm reminded to be compassionate with myself, knowing that tomorrow is another day and that I'm doing the best I can with what I have.

I hope this book finds a prominent place in your home to empower you in a similar way.

About the Publisher

The Dreamwork Collective is a print and digital publisher sharing diverse voices and powerful stories with the world. Dedicated to the advancement of humanity, we strive to create books that have a positive impact on people and on the planet. Our hope is that our books document this moment in time for future generations to enjoy and learn from, and that we play our part in ushering humanity into a new era of heightened creativity, connection, and compassion.

www.thedreamworkcollective.com
⊙ thedreamworkcollective